Yoroshiku
よろしく

Moshi Moshi
Teachers' Handbook

Stages 1 & 2

Yoroshiku was developed by the National Japanese Curriculum Project teams in Western Australia and Queensland.

PROJECT MANAGERS

Western Australia	*Queensland*
Jeanette Hasleby	Kerry Fairbairn
Pam Moss	Anna van Hoof

WRITERS

Western Australia	*Queensland*
Clare Buising	Deleece Batt
Naoko Homma	Bronwyn Dewar
Pam Moss	Peter Grainger
Peter Williams	Ros Story

Yoroshiku
よろしく

Moshi Moshi
Teachers' Handbook

Stages 1 & 2

もしもし

National Japanese Curriculum Project
Ministry of Education, Western Australia
Department of Education, Queensland

Curriculum
CORPORATION

Published by Curriculum Corporation
ACN 007 342 421
St Nicholas Place
141 Rathdowne St
Carlton Vic 3053
Australia
Tel: (03) 639 0699
Fax: (03) 639 1616

© Curriculum Corporation, 1993
Reprinted 1994

National Library of Australia
Cataloguing-in-publication data

Yoroshiku: moshi moshi. Teachers' handbook.

ISBN 1 86366 140 9.

1. Japanese language — Study and teaching (Secondary). 2.
Japanese language — Study and teaching (Secondary) — English
speakers. I. Queensland. Dept. of Education. II. Western Australia.
Ministry of Education. III. National Japanese Language Curriculum
Project (Australia). IV. Curriculum Corporation (Australia).
(Series: National Curriculum guidelines for Japanese, K-12).

495.60712

Edited by Margot Holden
Designed by Lauren Statham, Alice Graphics
Typeset in 11/13 pt Goudy and Mincho by Post Typesetters
Printed in Australia by Impact Printing

Foreword

The Asian Studies Council stated in its National Strategy that the study of Asia and its languages in Australian schools is about national survival in an intensely competitive world. To encourage learning of Asian languages in our schools, the Asian Studies Council in close cooperation with States, Territories and the Commonwealth, initiated major curriculum development.

The outcomes of this collaborative development are National Curriculum Guidelines for teaching and learning the Chinese, Japanese, Indonesian, Thai, Korean and Vietnamese languages. Informed by the *Australian Language Levels (ALL) Guidelines*, these materials provide comprehensive curriculum frameworks supported by teaching and learning resources. They provide important guidance on methodology, content and assessment attuned to student needs and supporting teacher confidence and competence.

The goal of the National Curriculum Guidelines for Asian Languages is communication in the language — integrating language learning and cultural information. The learning, teaching and planning outcomes are consonant with the National Curriculum Statement and Profile being developed collaboratively for LOTE.

Yoroshiku, meaning 'pleased to meet you', is the series title for National Curriculum Guidelines for Japanese. The *Yoroshiku* series is structured in three levels:

- *Niko Niko* Stages A & B — Early childhood to upper Primary
- *Moshi Moshi* Stages 1 & 2 — Lower to Middle Secondary
- *Pera Pera* Stages 3 & 4 — Senior Secondary.

Excellence in the content and design of *Yoroshiku* will be readily acknowledged by users — students and teachers alike. The project is timely, the development work imaginative and focused, and the presentation inspiring.

Yoroshiku materials will assume a very significant place in a concerned national effort to ensure we are more Asia aware, Asia literate and Asia involved.

David Francis
Executive Director
Curriculum Corporation

Project team acknowledgements

The National Japanese Curriculum Project was made possible due to substantial funding support from the Asian Studies Council, together with considerable administrative and curriculum writing support provided by the Queensland Department of Education and the Western Australian Ministry of Education. The Australia–Japan Foundation, in funding professional development workshops throughout Australia, has also played a key role in ensuring that the materials have an Australia-wide context. In particular, the writing team would like to acknowledge the many educators across Australia who have contributed their ideas, guidance and reactions to the materials which have been produced.

The central components of the National Curriculum Guidelines for Japanese, the Teachers' Handbooks, owe much to the *Australian Language Levels (ALL) Guidelines* for providing the fundamental organisational structure which the writers were able to adapt to suit the needs of Japanese teachers and learners in Australian schools. The writers are particularly grateful to the ALL Project team, in particular, Angela Scarino, David Vale and Penny McKay for their unstinting consultative guidance and inservice support.

Much appreciation is extended to the National Reference Group, chaired by Professor Alan Rix, (University of Queensland) and consisting of representatives from each State and Territory education authority: Brian Dooley and subsequently Helen Reid (ACT), Margaret Davidsohn and subsequently Inara Merrick (NSW), Ruza Ruzic and subsequently Carl Walker (NT), Kerry Fairbairn (Qld), Kostas Fotiadis (SA), Barrie Muir (Tas), Ruben Ketchell and subsequently Julie Riley (Vic), Gisela Birch and subsequently Pam Moss (WA), Marjan Ziemnicki (National Catholic Education Commission), Lorrie Maher (National Council of Independent Schools), Jim Wilson and Jenny Shapcott (Asian Studies Council), Lineke Spooner (DEET) and Angela Scarino (ALL Project). Advice from this body was instrumental in ensuring that the materials reflect the broad context of Japanese teaching and learning across Australia.

At a national level, the writers also acknowledge the valuable feedback provided by Professor David Ingram (Griffith University) in his mid-term evaluation of draft materials. Acknowledgement is also made of the contribution of Cathie Elder (National Languages and Literacy Institute of Australia) to the assessment component of the Teachers' Handbooks.

In Queensland and Western Australia, the writers acknowledge the ongoing support from their Project managers: Pam Moss and subsequently Jeanette Hasleby in Western Australia, Kerry Fairbairn and subsequently Anna van Hoof in Queensland. The writers are also grateful for the advice and support from groups of teachers in each State who have made invaluable comments on the draft materials. Other groups whose support and contribution is greatly appreciated are the members of the National Curriculum Projects in Chinese, Indonesian and Thai, and the following people: June Fox, Roger Gardiner, Lorraine Gentry, Haruo Ino, Takashi Sato, Tadayuki Takami and Hitoshi Yamashita.

Finally, the writers also wish to thank support staff in the Queensland Department of Education and the Western Australian Ministry of Education for their unending support and assistance.

Clare Buising

Naoko Homma

Pam Moss

Peter Williams

Deleece Batt

Bronwyn Dewar

Peter Grainger

Ros Story

Contents

Stage 1 modules

Stage 2 modules 85

Appendices 121

Learning Japanese

Rationale

The ability to use language effectively is an essential part of the educational process. As described in the *ALL Guidelines* (Book 1, page 1), learning a second language offers learners the potential to:

- communicate in the target language;
- enhance their intellectual and social development;
- enhance their understanding of their first language and culture;
- expand their knowledge and approach tasks with insights gained from another language and culture;
- participate in the life of another culture and gain an understanding of the similarities and differences between cultures;
- enhance their self-esteem;
- develop their sense of social justice;
- enhance their vocational prospects.

Apart from the cultural, intellectual and social benefits of language learning for the individual, languages are a valuable national resource which can serve communities within Australia, enrich Australian society as a whole, and enable the nation to engage in commercial, industrial and diplomatic enterprises on an international scale. Australians' knowledge of a language other than English and their understanding of the background culture can play a significant role in Australia's political and economic affairs.

As Australia's economic, cultural and educational contact with Japan assumes greater importance, and as Australia takes its place as a member of the Asian family of nations, the need for Australians, equipped with appropriate language skills and cultural awareness, becomes paramount. Effective Japanese language programs in our schools provide the foundation for young Australians to develop these understandings and skills.

Essential conditions

While it is true that the teacher of Japanese has a great deal of influence on whether or not the language program is successful, several factors, which are usually beyond the control of the teacher, are crucial to the success of the program, and are usually the province of the school's administrative body.

A favourable environment for learning Japanese has the following characteristics. These should be considered when language programs are being planned.

- a supportive school administration;
- a flexible timetabling arrangement with a sufficient number of regular exposures within that timetable to enable language competence to be developed. The following minimum allocations of time are considered appropriate:
  - *Early Childhood–Upper Primary* — two to three separate sessions per week;
  - *Lower Secondary* — three to four separate sessions per week;
  - *Upper Secondary* — daily sessions, totalling not less than 240 minutes per week;
- access for teachers and learners to appropriate material resources which will enable the program to be conducted effectively;
- an acceptable level of teaching competence in the spoken and written aspects of the Japanese language, e.g. the teacher can sustain accurate communication over a wide range of topics and contexts;
- a rich learning environment, preferably a classroom or an area of the classroom set aside for the learning of Japanese;
- assurance of continuity of language learning.

Getting to know the guidelines

Stages and pathways

The ALL Framework of Stages

The *ALL Guidelines* Framework of Stages (Book 1, page 32) is a series of progressive, interlocking, age-related Stages of language learning from early childhood to upper secondary LOTE (language other than English) learners. The Framework of Stages suggests ways in which the syllabus content of individual Stages may be linked to create pathways for language learning.

In a similar way to the ALL Framework of Stages, the organisational basis for the National Curriculum Guidelines for Japanese is the series of Stages represented in the table below. The Stages have been designed to provide a mechanism for facilitating continuity of Japanese learning between schools. In addition, the Stages provide schools with a common mechanism for describing and reporting learner achievement during their study of Japanese.

The Stages have been designed to allow for entry to Japanese learning at a number of key points: early childhood, primary and lower secondary. Upon completion of a Stage, learners will follow a pathway through the various Stages as represented in the table. It is expected that each Stage will be completed in two to four years at primary level, and in one to three years at secondary level. It is anticipated that learners will undertake Stage 4 in the senior year (Year 12).

Stage 1 is a beginning Stage for learners with no previous experience of Japanese. Stage 2 represents a continuation of Stage 1. Learners who have completed Stages A and B would be likely to proceed directly to Stage 2.

It should be noted that these Guidelines are not designed to cater for the needs of background speakers of Japanese.

	Year of schooling (varies by State)		Stages of the National Curriculum Guidelines for Japanese	
	Early childhood Primary Years 1–6 Secondary Years 7–12	*Early childhood Primary Years 1–7 Secondary Years 8–12*	*Early childhood and primary entry*	
Early childhood	K/P/R/1 2 3 4 5	K/P/R/1 2 3 4 5	Stage A and Stage B OR Stage B	*Lower secondary entry*
Primary	6	6,7		
Lower secondary	7 8 9 10	8 9 10	Stage 2 (and Stage 3)	Stage 1 and Stage 2
Upper secondary	11 12	11 12	Stage 3 and Stage 4	Stage 3 and Stage 4

Sample learning pathways

The following examples of learning pathways through the Stages show how the Stages might apply to various groups of learners. The length of a Stage will depend, for example, on the number of exposures per week, the general ability of learners and the general level of interest in Japanese.

The sample pathways suggest where it may be appropriate to introduce learners to material from more than one Stage.

Sample pathway 1: *Early childhood entry*

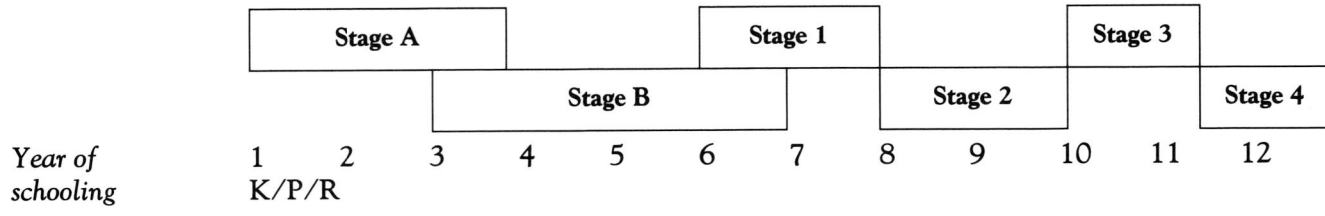

Stage A			Stage B				Stage 1		Stage 2	Stage 3	Stage 4

Year of schooling: 1 2 3 4 5 6 7 8 9 10 11 12
K/P/R

Sample pathway 2: *Early childhood entry*

Stage A			Stage B				Stage 1	Stage 2		Stage 3	Stage 4

Year of schooling: 1 2 3 4 5 6 7 8 9 10 11 12
K/P/R

Sample pathway 3: *Middle/upper primary entry*

| Stage A | | Stage B | | | | Stage 1 | Stage 2 | | Stage 3 | Stage 4 |

Year of schooling: 4 5 6 7 8 9 10 11 12

Sample pathway 4: *Lower secondary entry*

| Stage 1 | | Stage 2 | | Stage 3 | Stage 4 |

Year of schooling: 7 8 9 10 11 12

Sample pathway 5: *Lower secondary entry*

| Stage 1 | | Stage 2 | | Stage 3 | Stage 4 |

Year of schooling: 8 9 10 11 12

Stage 1 and Stage 2 target groups

As indicated in the sample pathways, the Stage 1 curriculum guidelines are intended for learners of Japanese who:

- are in lower secondary school;
- are beginning learners of Japanese;
- have had little or no previous contact with the Japanese language.

The Stage 2 curriculum guidelines are intended for learners of Japanese who:

- are in lower secondary school;
- have completed Stage 1;

  or

  have completed Stages A and B;

  or

  have completed Stage B only.

Goals

The focus and organisation of the National Curriculum Guidelines for Japanese are substantially underpinned by the principles of the *ALL Guidelines*, but modified to accommodate specific considerations for the teaching of Japanese, e.g. the introduction of script.

Following is a brief summary of the principles central to the *ALL Guidelines* and, thus, these curriculum guidelines.

Broad goals

In planning the general direction of LOTE programs, the *ALL Guidelines* identifies five broad categories of goals which are relevant to all language programs at every level of schooling (*ALL Guidelines*, Book 1, pages 29–31). Each broad category is described below. These categories should not be regarded as discrete, but as interrelated, with communication as the central goal as shown in the diagram opposite.

Communication goals
By participating in activities organised around the use of Japanese, learners will acquire communication skills in Japanese which will enable them to widen their networks of interpersonal relations, have direct access to information in Japanese and use their language skills for study, vocational and leisure-based purposes.

Socio-cultural goals
Learners will develop an understanding of Japanese culture which they can use as a basis for informed comparison with other cultures. They will thus develop an appreciation of the validity of the different ways of perceiving and encoding experience and of organising interpersonal relations, and reach a more secure acceptance of their personal identity and value. Learners will be able to understand more about Japanese culture and develop positive attitudes towards it.

Learning-how-to-learn goals
Learners will be able to take a growing responsibility for the management of their own learning, so that they learn how to learn, and how to learn a language.

Language and cultural awareness goals
Learners will reflect upon and develop an awareness of the role and nature of language and culture in everyday life, so that they may understand the diversity of the world around them and act appropriately.

General knowledge goals
Learners will gain knowledge and understanding of a range of subject matter related to their needs, interests and aspirations, as well as to other areas of their formal learning.

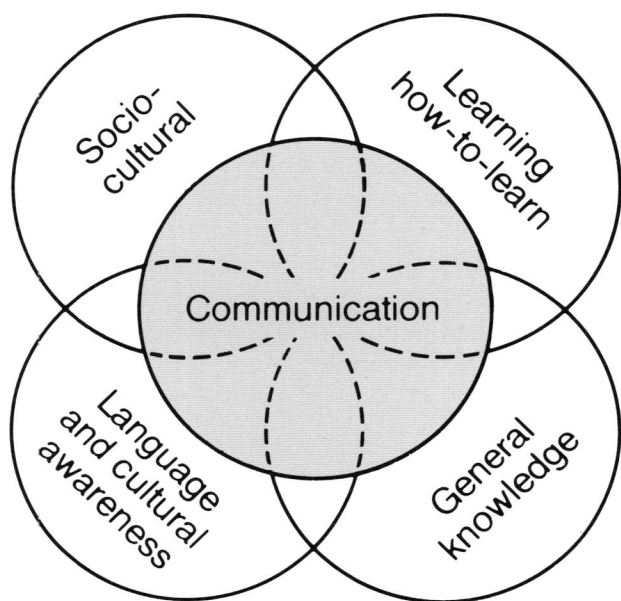

Fig. 1
Source: *ALL Guidelines*, Book 1, page 31

Specific goals

The *All Guidelines* (Book 2, page 18) has also identified a set of specific goals (derived from the previous broad goals) which bring the broad goals closer to what teachers might be aiming to promote in their LOTE programs:

Communication goals
To be able to use Japanese to:

- establish and maintain relationships and discuss topics of interest, e.g. through the exchange of information, ideas, opinions, attitudes, feelings, experiences and plans;

- participate in social interaction related to solving a problem, making arrangements, making decisions with others, and transacting to obtain goods, services and public information;
- obtain information by searching for specific details in a spoken or written text, then process and use the information obtained;
- obtain information by listening to or reading a spoken or written text as a whole, then process and use the information obtained;
- give information in spoken or written form, e.g. give a talk, write a short passage or set of instructions;
- listen to, read or view, and respond personally to a stimulus, e.g. a story, play, film, song, poem, picture;
- be involved in spoken or written personal expression, e.g. create a story, dramatic episode, poem, play.

Socio-cultural goals

To develop an appropriate level of knowledge and understanding of the following aspects of the Japanese community:

- how interpersonal relations are conducted;
- everyday life patterns of the contemporary age group of the learner;
- cultural traditions; dress, festivals, songs, games, dancing, folk stories, family structure;
- historical roots and relationships to other communities; geographical features of Japan;
- the economy and the world of work;
- political and social institutions;
- cultural achievements;
- current affairs.

Learning-how-to-learn goals

To develop:

- cognitive processing skills (to enable the learner to understand and express values, attributes and feelings; to process information, and to think and respond creatively);
- learning-how-to-learn skills (to enable learners to take responsibility for their own learning);
- communication strategies (to enable the learner to sustain communication in Japanese).

The *ALL Guidelines* also contains examples of the skills and strategies related to the learning-how-to-learn goals (Book 2, Appendix 1).

Language and cultural awareness goals

To develop an understanding of:

- the aesthetic features in the learner's own language and in the language of others;
- the functions of language in everyday life;
- the systematic nature of language and how it works;
- the way that language adapts to context;
- the concepts of accent, dialect, register and other forms of language variation:
- how language grows, borrows, changes, falls into disuse and dies;
- how language is learnt (both as a first and as a second language);
- how language is a manifestation of culture;
- cultural variation and the enriching nature of diversity;
- the importance of language maintenance to members of a language's speech community.

General knowledge goals

General knowledge goals apply to all programs to varying degrees and will largely depend upon the characteristics of the particular learner group.

The place of goals

Broad goals and specific goals provide a general direction for teaching and learning Japanese. Some implications of the goals, namely how they suggest what learners will be able to *do*, are described in the chapter on general objectives.

The activities-based approach

Rationale

It is suggested that teachers adopt an approach to teaching Japanese based on the eight principles of teaching and learning identified in the *ALL Guidelines* (Book 1, page 17). Learners learn a language best when:

1. they are treated as individuals with their own needs and interests
2. they are provided with opportunities to participate in communicative use of the target language in a wide range of activities
3. they are exposed to communicative data which is comprehensible and relevant to their own needs and interests
4. they focus deliberately on various language forms, skills and strategies in order to support the process of language acquisition
5. they are exposed to sociocultural data and direct experience of the culture embedded within the target language
6. they become aware of the role and nature of language and culture
7. they are provided with appropriate feedback about their progress
8. they are provided with opportunities to manage their own learning.

Therefore, learners are most likely to benefit from a methodology which:

- is learner-centred;
- encourages the maximum purposeful use of Japanese in meaningful contexts;
- allows for instruction on particular language elements, skills and strategies to support learning.

Teaching methodology — activities and exercises

Based on this rationale, the approach recommended is an activities-based approach, where the activity is seen as the central focus of teaching and learning. In the *ALL Guidelines* (Book 2, page 19), an activity is defined as follows:

> An activity involves the purposeful and active use of language where learners are required to call upon their language resource to meet the needs of a given communicative situation.

This implies that activities involve *use* of listening, speaking, reading and writing skills (in different combinations) *to achieve a purpose* such as personal interaction, the sharing of information or personal expression. The definition also implies that in order to successfully participate in activities, learners require the foundations of language knowledge, communication strategies and an understanding of the culture and values of the Japanese language community.

A key foundation in a learner's ability to participate in activities is knowledge of the elements of language such as functions, notions, grammar, syntax and vocabulary. Such a grounding can be developed by presenting learners with opportunities for language practice, such as drills, word games, pattern practice, etc. As in the *ALL Guidelines*, classroom procedures which focus on language practice are referred to as exercises. The *ALL Guidelines* (Book 2, page 19) defines exercises as follows:

> An exercise focuses on one or more elements of the communication process in order to promote learning of the items of language, knowledge, skills and strategies needed in communication activities.

As it is possible to provide learners with a wide range of activities, it is also possible to provide a wide range of exercises. A number of exercise types have been suggested for use with these curriculum guidelines and these are described more fully on page 32.

The planning and monitoring of the range, grouping and sequencing of activities and exercises is a fundamental consideration in the use of these curriculum guidelines and is discussed in more detail in 'Planning a unit of work' on page 30.

General objectives

The place of general objectives

Whereas the goals of language learning (on page 10) elaborate the *direction* of teaching and learning in these curriculum guidelines, the *general objectives describe what learners will be able to do* with what they have learnt.

The general objectives below are a summary of what learners will be able to do using the range of language content suggested for Stage 1 and Stage 2 (see pages 20–23). More detailed descriptions of what learners might be able to do and the language they might require, are contained in the modules.

General objectives for Stage 1

Within the range of language content introduced in Stage 1, learners can be considered to have satisfactorily completed Stage 1 when they can perform the following tasks:

Interpersonal use of language
* follow short spoken classroom instructions;
* use a variety of everyday expressions and responses (e.g. greetings);
* introduce themselves and other learners;
* ask and answer short, well-rehearsed questions about familiar, everyday topics (e.g. in order to make arrangements);
* engage in and sustain a short conversation about a simple familiar theme;
* develop and present short role-plays and skits with a small number of participants involving manipulation of familiar sentences;
* write short letters and journals about familiar topics.

Informational use of language
* listen to short spoken presentations to extract simple specific items of information;
* listen to short spoken presentations and write short summaries (e.g. lists) of the information given;
* listen to short spoken presentations about familiar topics and extract the overall gist;
* give short spoken presentations about familiar everyday topics using well-rehearsed sentences (e.g. with supporting photos or pictures);

* read simple short letters, notes, messages, menus, neighbourhood signs, store guides and simple TV guides containing familiar words in hiragana and katakana to extract specific items of information;
* write short lists;
* write short captions (e.g. for a poster about free time);
* write short passages in hiragana and katakana giving simple information (e.g. a TV program review).

Aesthetic use of language
* write short creative passages including simple descriptions (e.g. of an ideal house);
* write short poems and imaginative accounts (e.g. of a seasonal activity);
* write short passages to promote something (e.g. a simple advertisement).

Script
* recognise and write all hiragana;
* recognise all katakana;
* write familiar words in katakana;
* recognise (but not necessarily write) a range of kanji, as appropriate.

During Stage 1, learners will acquire the ability to use hiragana and katakana gradually. For this reason, the Stage 1 module objectives include a number of script objectives or script 'benchmarks' which learners might be expected to be able to achieve.

General objectives for Stage 2

Within the range of language content introduced in Stage 2, learners can be considered to have satisfactorily completed Stage 2 when they can perform the following tasks.

Interpersonal use of language
* engage in and sustain short conversations around a range of familiar themes;
* develop and present 1–2 minute role-plays and skits with a small number of participants based around familiar themes, topics and situations;
* listen to or watch a spoken presentation (e.g. a role-play) and make a short spoken response;
* ask and answer 'quiz' questions about simple

general knowledge topics (e.g. Australia and Japan);
- read short letters and journals about familiar topics and write brief notes, messages and short letters in response;
- write short letters and journals about familiar topics (e.g. with supporting information such as maps, photos, simple explanations);
- write brief messages and notes for someone (e.g. where and how to feed a pet).

Informational use of language
- listen to short spoken texts to extract several specific items of information;
- listen to short spoken passages of information and write short summaries;
- listen to a variety of spoken texts about familiar topics, containing a small number of unfamiliar words, and identify the overall gist;
- give short spoken presentations about familiar themes, topics and situations;
- read a variety of simple texts in hiragana, katakana and kanji, and extract specific items of information;
- read a variety of simple texts in hiragana, katakana and kanji, including a small number of unfamiliar words, and identify the overall gist;
- write short informative passages in hiragana, katakana and a number of simple kanji (e.g. explanatory notes to accompany a map of the school);
- write simple maps, posters and menus.

Aesthetic use of language
- write simple personal responses to pictures and photos;
- write descriptive paragraphs to promote something (e.g. a product, a shop);
- write short poems (e.g. a *cinquain* poem).

Script
- recognise and write a range of kanji, as appropriate.

Learner performance

The descriptions which follow are intended as a guide to expected learner performance in Stage 1 and Stage 2. For example, in Stage 1, learners' language will generally comprise well-rehearsed and frequently used sentences. By Stage 2, it is anticipated that learners will be able to cope with a range of themes and topics, changes of topic in a conversation, for example, and small amounts of unpredictable language. However, they will generally require support in the form of repetition, paraphrasing and/or gestures in order to do so.

The descriptions also suggest *how much* learners are likely to understand and *how well* they are likely to be able to perform. This information may assist teachers when assessing learners' performance through observation or more formal assessment procedures.

When reading these descriptions it is important to bear in mind that they serve as a guide only.

Stage 1 performance characteristics

In general, learners in Stage 1 are likely to:

- produce short spoken sentences based around a small number of predictable, high-frequency contexts;
- use short patterns with simple substitutions;
- experiment with guessing the meaning of unfamiliar or unpredictable words where support is provided (e.g. through repetition, gestures, miming, teacher encouragement);
- use all hiragana (there may be difficulties with some combinations, e.g. ちょっと and しゅくだい);
- use a small number of high-frequency katakana words and experiment with less familiar words

where support is provided (e.g. contextual clues, teacher and peer assistance);
- recognise and write a small number of frequently used kanji (learners will generally be able to recognise, or partially recognise, a larger number of kanji than they are able to write);
- produce written sentences where these are frequently used and well-practised, although some learners may rely on guides and models when writing.

Stage 2 performance characteristics

In general, learners in Stage 2 are likely to:

- sustain conversations around simple themes;
- cope with changes in theme, topic and speaker (e.g. in conversations) where these are clear;
- manipulate a variety of patterns with a range of substitutions and simple cohesive devices (e.g. linking words, simple contrasts);
- cope with small amounts of unfamiliar or unpredictable language where support is provided (e.g. contextual clues, repetition, gestures);
- cope with speakers of Japanese other than their teacher, where the person speaks clearly and deliberately;
- participate in simple group decisions involving a number of variables (e.g. who, when, how);
- understand and use all hiragana and frequently used katakana combinations although decoding of written material for some learners may remain slow;
- recognise and write frequently used kanji (learners will generally be able to recognise, or partially recognise, a larger number of kanji than they are able to write).

The modules

The modules for each Stage (see pages 49–119) are organised into the following components:

- module objectives
- suggested activities
- other learning experiences
- suggested units of work
- module checklists (language content)
- suggested kanji for recognition

These sections are explained below.

Module objectives

Whereas the general objectives summarise what learners will be able to do on completion of a Stage, the module objectives provide descriptions of expected learner achievement over a shorter term, e.g. over several lessons, at the end of a module. The module objectives therefore play an important role in assessment — an issue discussed more fully in the chapter on assessment.

The module objectives are described in terms of a number of elements:

- *a mode of language use*, e.g. give a talk, understand a sign, ask and answer questions;
- *an indication of language content*, e.g. a weekend outing, pets, after-school interests;
- *an indication of the level of expected performance*, e.g. a short conversation containing three to four items of well-rehearsed information.

The following module objectives (from Stage 1, Module 5) illustrate how these elements can be integrated.

Learners will be able to:
- *listen to short spoken passages for several items of simple information about the neighbourhood, e.g. home, favourite places, location;*
- *engage in and sustain a simple conversation about the neighbourhood.*

Focusing on the elements of a module objective can help make explicit the kinds of purposeful language activities which will enable learners to achieve the objective. For example, the first of the above module objectives suggests the following activities.

- *interviewing each other to find popular places in the neighbourhood and marking them on a map;*

- *asking friends about places in the local area, which attractions they like and dislike;*
- *completing a survey sheet.*

The module objectives therefore indicate a range of possible activities, examples of which are provided in each module. The selection of module objectives and activities to meet those objectives is a major consideration when planning a series of lessons and is referred to in the section, 'Developing a unit of work' on page 33.

Suggested activities

As described in the chapter, 'The activities-based approach', these curriculum guidelines place activities as the central focus of teaching, learning and assessment. Activities involve doing something purposeful with language in order to meet the needs of a communicative situation, e.g. answering a series of interview questions, completing a survey sheet or writing a poster caption.

Each module presents a range of suggested activities related to the module title and suggested units of work. Within each module, activities are broadly categorised in terms of *three dimensions of language use:*

- *Interpersonal dimension*, involving a focus on interpersonal relationships and exchanges, e.g. conversations, exchanges of correspondence;
- *Informational dimension*, involving a focus on acquiring and processing information from public sources, e.g. finding information from brochures or timetables, labelling a set of directions;
- *Aesthetic dimension*, involving a focus on creative or imaginative use of language, e.g. a poster caption, a talk about how the school environment could be improved.

Within each dimension, activities can also be categorised into more specific *activity-types*, represented as follows.

Interpersonal dimension
- **Activity-type 1:** Interacting and discussing topics of interest, e.g. ideas, experiences;
- **Activity-type 2:** Interacting to get things done, e.g. solving a problem, making arrangements.

Informational dimension

- **Activity-type 3:** Obtaining information and using it, e.g. listening to a weather forecast and selecting what to wear;
- **Activity-type 4:** Giving information, e.g. a talk about a holiday outing.

Aesthetic dimension

- **Activity-type 5:** Making a personal response, e.g. to a video program, to a picture;
- **Activity-type 6:** Personal expression, e.g. writing a poem, performing a skit.

While the broad focus of activities can be represented by one of the above activity-types, activities may often involve more than one dimension or activity-type. For example, an activity such as 'presenting a skit featuring ordering a meal at a restaurant' (activity-type 6)

may involve 'gaining the attention of the waiter' (activity-type 1), 'searching for information from a menu' (activity-type 3), 'deciding with a friend what to eat and placing an order' (activity-type 2).

The dimensions and activity-types are not therefore seen as 'watertight compartments' but as mechanisms for planning and monitoring the spread of activities over a period of time. The dimensions and activity-types are represented in the Table of Language Use, as described in the *ALL Guidelines* (Book 2, page 22).

As discussed previously, the choice of individual activities will be strongly influenced by the module objectives. In order to meet particular module objectives, teachers may wish to select from the suggested activities and adapt others. It will not normally be practical to use all the activities in a particular module.

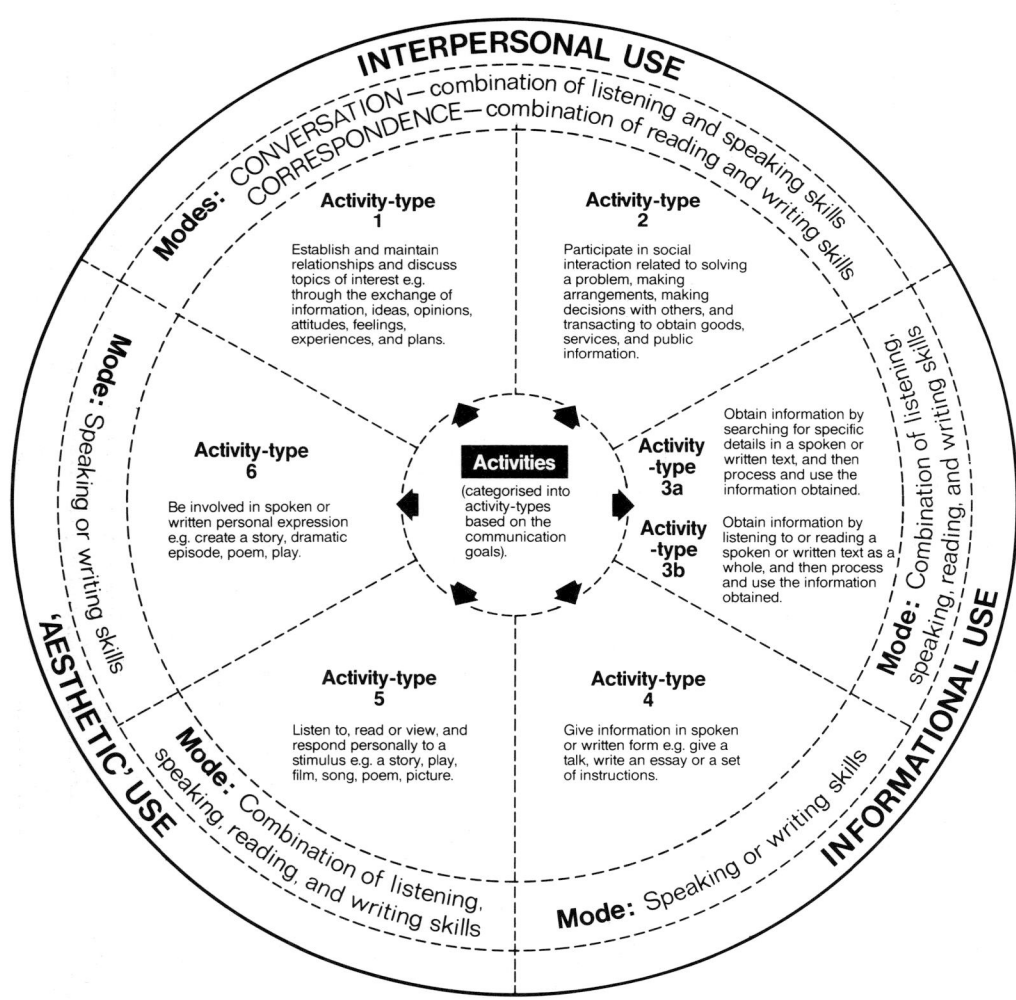

Fig. 2 Table of language use

Source: Scarino, A., Vale, D., McKay, P. & Clarke, J. *Australian Language Levels (ALL) Guidelines*. Canberra, Curriculum Development Centre, 1988.

Symbols accompanying many of the suggested activities indicate related material in the *Teachers' Resources* (blackline masters) and the *Student Book*.

The selection of activities (and the selection and teaching of language needed by learners for the activities) is elaborated in the sections 'Selecting activities' on page 30 and 'Selecting language for an activity' on page 31.

Further information about the use of activity-types is elaborated in the *ALL Guidelines* (Book 2, pages 21–26).

Other learning experiences

At certain points in the teaching and learning program, it may be appropriate to focus on one or more sociocultural, learning-how-to-learn or language and cultural awareness items, e.g. discussing the clubs and activities open to students in Japanese schools, teaching how to scan a piece of written text for important details or how one verb form may differ from another. These focuses can typically occur before, during or after the language activity, and are referred to in the modules as 'other learning experiences'.

The number of other learning experiences which can arise in a module is potentially unlimited. A small number of these is suggested in each module.

While a focus on other learning experiences may provide an interesting 'diversion' in the learning program, it is recommended that they be integrated as much as possible with the suggested activities described in the modules.

Some other learning experiences will lend themselves to being conducted in English, while others may require Japanese and are suggested as other learning experiences because they may not be directly related to one of the six activity-types. Useful other learning experiences — not specifically related to Japanese — can be found in *Stage 1 of a K–12 Series of Syllabus Exemplars: Italian*, page 39, and can be readily adapted to a Japanese teaching and learning setting.

The inclusion of other learning experiences in the learning program is further discussed in the section, 'Developing a unit of work', on page 33.

Suggested units of work

For organisational reasons and as a means of building variety into a module, it is recommended that modules be broken down into smaller, more compact 'units'. For example, a module entitled 'Neighbourhoods' (Stage 1, Module 5) could comprise a group of lessons focused on the learners' home environments, followed by a focus on the neighbourhood, followed by a short, specific focus on reading maps and signs. These focuses provide a means of clustering related activities and are referred to in the modules as units of work.

A small number of suggested units of work is provided in each module. As with the suggested activities, the suggested units of work may require adaptation for particular groups of learners and situations. Catchy, interesting or appealing unit of work titles can be a powerful tool for focusing learners' attention over a number of lessons. However units of work which do not appear to connect or integrate a series of activities can have a negative impact on learning.

A suggested method of using units of work is discussed in the section, 'Developing a unit of work', on page 33.

Module checklists

In order to participate successfully in activities from the modules, learners will need to be familiar with a range of language exponents. A selection of those considered relevant for each module is provided in the module checklists. (For an indication of the range of language exponents presented in each Stage, teachers should refer to the summaries of suggested language content on pages 20–23.)

The language exponents in the module checklists are derived from the language functions and notions suggested by the module objectives. The checklists also indicate the types of language exponents learners are likely to encounter in the resources developed to support these curriculum guidelines.

The exponents provided in the checklists are not seen as the only ones to teach or the 'best' ones for every activity in the module. Some exponents may require adaptation for a particular group of learners or for a particular activity.

For information on one approach for selecting language exponents for activities, refer to page 31. Information on how learners might be introduced to language exponents is given in the section, 'Introducing and practising language', on page 32.

Kanji for recognition

The kanji for recognition included in the modules are suggestions only. Refer also to the section, 'Introducing kanji for recognition', on page 29.

Language content

The summaries of suggested language content which follow for Stage 1 and Stage 2 are drawn from the checklists which follow each module. These summaries give an indication of the language which will support the activities described in the modules.

The summaries are intended to be guides only and not prescriptive lists. Teachers may wish to add or delete language as appropriate to particular teaching and learning circumstances, e.g. the choice of module objectives, the age and interests of learners, the level of learners' exposure to Japanese.

The suggested language is presented as:

- a summary of language functions
- a summary of language notions
- a summary of language exponents
- a summary of suggested script.

Language functions

The various ways learners may be required to *use* language in order to participate in activities are described as language functions. For example, during a shopping scene role-play, learners may be required to:

- *enquire about* (availability);
- *give information* (about price); and
- *request* (a quantity of goods).

Enquiring about, *giving information* and *requesting* are examples of Stage 1 and Stage 2 language functions.

Language notions

While language functions describe how the language is being used, language notions describe what is being talked or written *about*. For example during a role-play, learners may be enquiring about and giving information about:

- *availability* and
- *price*;

and requesting a

- *quantity of goods*.

Availability, *price* and *quantity of goods* are examples of Stage 1 and Stage 2 language notions.

Language exponents

Language functions and notion combine to suggest language exponents (which contain essential grammar and vocabulary). For example, during a role-play, learners may be required to *enquire about availability* and *give information about price*. Learners may therefore need to be familiar with the following language exponents (and grammar):

- Ｔシャツがありますか。
  （はい、あります。）
- （あかいＴシャツはいくらですか。）
  八百円です。

The examples given are presented in their polite form. Teachers are encouraged to introduce less formal equivalents at appropriate times.

Suggested script

It is recommended that learners are made aware of the existence of kanji. Teachers are encouraged to select a small number of relevant, interesting or simple kanji for learners to recognise.

Suggested language content

Language functions

Socialising

introducing self and others
greeting others
using different modes of address
leavetaking
enquiring about health
interacting (in a shop)
identifying self (on the telephone)
responding (to roll call, apology, thanks)

Exchanging information

asking for and giving information
identifying
describing
agreeing and disagreeing
asking for and giving reasons
enquiring about and expressing likes and dislikes
enquiring about and expressing wishes
asking for reciprocal information
expressing ownership
making comparisons
expressing possibility

Expressing attitudes and feelings

apologising
thanking
approving
exclaiming
expressing surprise
congratulating
expressing opinions
expressing desire

Organising and maintaining communication

asking for repetition
seeking and giving confirmation
attracting attention
expressing lack of comprehension
asking how to say something
confirming information
emphasising opinions

Getting things done

asking for, giving and denying permission
making a request
offering help/advice
making suggestions
giving instructions and responding to instructions
making arrangements

Language notions

Personal identification

name
age
residence
nationality
telephone number
family and friends
birth date and birth sign
pets
greetings
introductions
likes and dislikes
favourites
year of schooling
hobbies

Leisure

weekend, holiday and leisure activities
TV programs
personalities
music

Eating and drinking

common foods and drinks
menus
restaurants and shops

Daily routines

clock time
days and dates
places
location
transport
frequency

Weather

season
weather forecasts
temperature

Shopping

shops
price
availability

Schooling

subjects
students and teachers
sports
travel to and from school

Other general notions

duration
degree
quantity
numbers (e.g. classifiers for people, animals)
amount
characteristics
purpose
physical appearance
truth and falsehood
correctness and incorrectness
taste
objects
ownership

Language exponents

Verb forms	Examples
～ます	うみへ行きます。
～ました	日本からきました。
～ませんでした	まちに行きませんでした。
～なさい	もうけしなさい！
～ています。	きょうとにすんでいます。
～ていません	びじゅつをべんきょうして いません。
～て	すわってください。
	すわって！
～てもいい	えいがを見てもいいです。
～てはだめ	見てはだめです。
～ません	うみに行きません。
～たい	りょこうをしたいです。
～たくない	べんきょうをしたくないです。
～ましょう	ジュースをのみましょう。

Copula	Examples
です	メリーです。
でしょう	あめでしょう。

Interrogatives	Examples
なん	何さいですか。
	何で行きますか。
なに	何どしですか。
どこ	どこにすんでいますか。
だれ	これはだれのですか。
どんな	しゅうまつにどんなスポーツを しましたか。
どの	どのぐらい日本語をべんきょう していますか。
どれ	どれがやすいですか。
どちら	どちらが好きですか。
どう	しゅうまつはどうでしたか。
	どうやって行きますか。
いつ	いつかいものに行きますか。
なぜ	なぜ好きですか。
いくら	いくらですか。
いくつ	いくつですか。

Particles	Examples
は	ジョンさんは？
	私はメリーです。
に	みせに行きました。
	みぎにあります。
	土曜日に行きます。
	あそびに行きます。
で	日本語でこたえてください。
	スーパーでかいものをします。
	5チャンネルでやっています。
を	本をあけてください。
と	おねえさんとわたしです。
	ともだちと行きます。
の	犬の名前は「クロ」です。
	えきの前です。
が	みかんが好きです。
も	すいえいも好きです。
へ	うみへ行きます。
から	キャンプはいつからですか。
まで	キャンプは土曜日までです。

Sentence final particles	Examples
か	どこに行きますか。
ね	それはいいですね。
よ	そうですよ。

Adjective forms	Examples
～い	犬は小さいです。
～かった	たのしかったです。
～くない	へやは大きくないです。
～じゃない	好きじゃないです。
～ではありません	好きではありません。
～じゃありません	好きじゃありません。
～です	テニスはだめです。

Adverb forms	Examples
ときどき	ときどきプールに行きます。
まいにち	まいにちバスで行きます。
よく	よくスポーツをします。
いちばん	一ばん好きなのみものは何 ですか。
ちょっと	ちょっと小さいです。
とても	こうえんはとても大きいです。
もう	日本は、もうつゆのきせつ ですか。
まだ	まだつゆじゃないです。
また	またどうぞ。

Demonstratives	Example
これ／それ	これはおいしいです。

Conjunctions	Examples
から	たのしいからです。
だから	だめだからです。
でも	いいお天気です。でも、 ちょっとさむいです。
じゃ	じゃ、そうしましょう。

Kanji for recognition

一 二 三 四 五 六 七 八 九 十 人 天 気 円 行 口 百 休 学 校 曜 家
大 小 名 前 本 語 新 私 犬 好 日 見 聞 書 入 出 時 中 先 生 年
月 火 水 木 金 土 何 春 夏 秋 冬

Suggested language content

Language functions*

Socialising
identifying self
introducing self and others
greeting others
responding (e.g. to greetings)
welcoming and farewelling

Exchanging information
asking for and giving information
making comparisons
narrating a sequence of events
describing people and things
enquiring about and expressing
    particular likes and dislikes
asking for and giving reasons
asking for and giving impressions
asking for and describing plans

asking for and describing actions
enquiring about and expressing
    capabilities
enquiring about and expressing
    wishes
enquiring about and expressing
    preferences
making predictions (about the
    weather)
asking for and giving directions
describing similarities and differences
identifying things and places

Getting things done
making arrangements
making suggestions
agreeing and disagreeing with
    suggestions

requesting
asking for, giving and denying
    permission
giving explanations
describing what is not allowed
reminding

Expressing attitudes and feelings
expressing desire
expressing surprise
expressing enjoyment

Organising and maintaining communication
hesitating
quoting direct speech

Language notions*

Personal Identification
physical characteristics
zodiac birth sign
character traits
personal interests
capabilities
achievements
future career
date of birth
birthplace
clothing

Eating and drinking
foods and drinks
menus
places where people eat
mealtimes
mealtime duties

Leisure
weekend and holiday activities
holiday travel
school holidays
leisure interests
sports
favourites
outings
things to take on outings

Schooling
schools in Australia and Japan

subjects
travel to and from school
shape of the school day
extra-curricula activities
clubs and teams
areas of the school
school buildings
school events
number in school

Daily routines
getting up
going to bed
meals
homework
hours and minutes
travel
daily expenses
after-school activities
money and pocket money
part-time jobs
savings

Shopping
price
purchases
availability

Home
rooms
other areas in the home

activities at home
home contents
things allowed at home
visitors
Japanese homes

Local area
shops and facilities
directions
distances

Weather
descriptions of the weather
weather forecasts
temperatures
seasonal activities

Environment
geographical areas
city and country
capital cities
states

Other general notions
duration
colour
degree of skill
completion
sequence
location
frequency (e.g. weekly, monthly)

*The functions and notions above are generally being introduced for the first time in Stage 2. Repetition of some Stage 1 functions and notions indicates further development in Stage 2.

Language exponents

Verb forms	Examples
pl. (plain form) 事	ダンスをする事が好きです。
pl. でしょう	あつくなるでしょう。
pl. つもり	りょこうするつもりです。
pl. 事にしました	りょこうに行く事にしました。
～ないで	ここで食べないでください。
～たほうがいい	ここで食べたほうがいいです。
～てもいい	パーティーに行ってもいいですか。
～てはいけません。	行ってはいけません。
～ていません	まだ食べていません。

Copula	Examples
でしょうか	あしたのお天気はどうでしょうか。

Interrogatives	Examples
なん	何さいですか。
どう	どうやって来ますか。

Particles	Examples
に	パイロットになります。
	りょうしんにもらいました。
	どこにも行きません。
も	どちらも好きです。
	何もしません。
で	ぜんぶでいくらですか。
	しんじゅで有名です。
や	英語や日本語を勉強しています。
が	たいふうが来ます。
	しゅくだいがおおいからです。
と	学校の名前は何と言いますか。
	へんだと思います。
	「～」と言いました。

	Examples
など	ふくやカセットなどを買いました。
は	ちょうれいの時は話してはいけません。

Phrases	Examples
たり	テレビを見たり、買い物に行ったりします。
～事ができます	行く事ができません。

Adjective forms	Examples
～い	赤いネクタイをしています。
～くて	あしがながくて目が茶色です。
～く	あたたかくなります。

Adverb forms	Examples
すこし／ちょっと	すこし／ちょっと下手です。
ぜんぜん	ぜんぜんできません。
だんだん	だんだんあつくなるでしょう。
すごく	12月はすごくあつかったです。
ほんとうに	ほんとうにおもしろいです。

Conjunctions	Examples
～て	あしがながくて目が茶色です。
	八時にはじまって、三時におわります。
で	さる年でおひつじざです。
	しんせつでおもしろいです。
そして	そして家にかえりました。
それから	それから食事をしました。
まず	まず、何をしましたか。
さいごに	さいごにバスでかえりました。
から	おもしろくないからです。
	しんせつじゃないからです。

Kanji for recognition

手 飲 都 客 楽
下 物 東 正 字
上 買 海 年 漢
青 言 茶 先 有
赤 分 強 今 毎
黒 天 勉 目 話
色 雨 左 週 思
茶 来 右 士 所
高々 館 富 住 英
耳 時 図 山 町 食
口 事 気 京 道 病

Using the guidelines

Key aspects of teaching and learning Japanese

Developing listening and speaking skills

As with other LOTE learners, learners of Japanese will generally be able to listen and understand more than they are able to 'say'. This gap between the level of development of understanding skills and speaking skills has implications for teaching and learning. Some of these are listed below.

- The optimum amount of vocabulary and grammar to introduce in a lesson is, ideally, an amount just beyond learners' reach, as this is most likely to maintain their interest and maximise their language development.
- Real communication will always contain an element of unpredictable language. If learners are exposed to manageable amounts of unpredictable language, they will develop valuable guessing skills and strategic skills (e.g. asking for clarification and repetition), and their comprehension.
- Language activities which focus on listening for understanding can be a little more demanding than activities which focus on speaking skills, e.g. they can contain slightly longer and more complex sentences and a greater number of less familiar words. The nature of what constitutes 'slightly longer' and 'more complex' will, of course, vary from group to group. However, teachers are encouraged to experiment with challenging learners in this way. This distinction between understanding skills and productive skills can also be applied to reading and writing tasks.
- Exposing learners to a variety of speakers of Japanese (e.g. through recorded audio and video tapes, visitors, exchange students) can help broaden learners' vocabulary and increase their tolerance of variation and diversity among speakers of Japanese.

Introducing script: a gradual process

For many learners of Japanese, the scripts are one of the most appealing and interesting aspects of their language learning. With the development of innovative approaches to learning kana such as *Hiragana in 48 Minutes* and other variations, learners can acquire a very basic level of competency in the recognition of hiragana (or katakana, as appropriate) in a very short time. For learners, this is a significant and exciting achievement. For teachers, the introduction of script can be a challenging and rewarding task, and it can be problematic.

In general, these curriculum guidelines recommend a *gradual approach* to the teaching of script where:

- script reinforces spoken language;
- script is used in ways which are interesting and manageable, with gradually increasing levels of demand;
- (for teachers) distinctions are made between the skills of 'recognition', 'reading for understanding', 'limited reproduction' and 'writing'.

The sections which follow address the above issues and suggest strategies which may assist teachers when introducing script.

First steps with hiragana: developing recognition skills

Mnemonic strategies such as those used in *Hiragana in 48 Minutes* can equip learners with a rudimentary competence in hiragana in a very short time. The mnemonic technique teaches recognition of single hiragana (or katakana or kanji) by visual association with a familiar English concept, word or phrase. For example, a teacher might say 'The hiragana よ looks like a yacht in the water and is called "yo". Everyone look at this hiragana and say "yo".'

The following strategies may assist teachers when planning introductory script lessons.

- Spend one or two lessons using a mnemonic technique such as *Hiragana in 48 Minutes* (or other variation).
- Follow up this lesson with tasks such as:
  - selecting a familiar word on a page of text and finding the number of times the word appears on the page;
  - selecting a common word-ending (or

beginning), e.g. ます、です, and finding the number of words on a page which contain that combination;
- playing dictionary games, e.g. identifying the first word on a particular page of the dictionary.

While there is nothing to stop learners beginning to write simple familiar words as early as possible, most learners will need much practice with recognition before developing sufficient confidence to begin to learn to write. For this reason, throughout Stages A, B and 1, the module objectives contain *script objectives* which represent a number of progressive script 'benchmarks' during a Stage and script 'targets' by the end of the Stage (Stages A and B, and Stage 1). The script objectives are phased out as the ability to make more purposeful use of hiragana/katakana develops; script objectives are then incorporated with the module objectives.

From recognition to reading

Once learners are able to recognise all or part of frequently used words, it is recommended that they be given some simple reading exercises. The following strategies may be helpful for learners:

- reading aloud small pieces of text with teacher support;
- pointing to words as they are read aloud by the teacher or other members of the class.

Reading strategies should include reading for understanding, e.g.:

- underlining key words in sentences;
- suggesting what the missing word in a sentence might be;
- deciding whether a sentence is true or false;
- joining:
  - single hiragana to form meaningful words;
  - a group of words to form a meaningful sentence;
  - a group of short sentences to form a meaningful paragraph;
- selecting which of two or more sentences best suits a picture;
- selecting which of two or more sentences best answers a question.

Introducing writing

It is often the case that learners themselves will indicate when they want to write Japanese. Teachers may find the following suggestions useful when writing skills are introduced.

- Approach writing by way of three incremental steps:
  1. limited reproduction, e.g. moulding single kana characters with playdough or pipe cleaners, tracing kana words, copying kana sentences;
  2. guided writing, e.g. filling in the missing parts of sentences and short paragraphs;
  3. free writing, e.g. writing short answers to questions, writing short pieces of information.
- Focus, initially, on language which is very familiar, either word-by-word, e.g. ねこ、いぬ、すきです, or character-by-character, e.g. あ、い、う、え、お、か、き.

It is well known that learners will take some time to be able to write Japanese scripts. However, this does not mean that learners should be 'sheltered' or withheld from script until they can write. While learners are mastering the writing of script, e.g. character-by-character or word-by-word, they can be using script in many ways which require little or no actual writing (see the strategies suggested in this chapter). It is important to acknowledge that time spent using or teaching romaji is time which could be spent developing valuable recognition and reading skills using authentic Japanese scripts. However subtle the use of romaji, e.g. to write 'important' words on the board, this gives romaji a defacto status which may be difficult to reverse.

In summary, for learners to acquire script skills quickly, they must see the need for using script and have opportunities to develop script skills in contexts which they can manage. The gradual approach suggested in this chapter is exemplified in the modules (and their related resources) and can be applied in most teaching and learning situations.

Introducing katakana

In general, these curriculum guidelines suggest an approach where hiragana is introduced first, followed by katakana and kanji. This does not mean that learners should avoid contact with katakana until they can confidently write in hiragana. For example, there may be great value in teaching learners to recognise a small number of frequently used words in katakana as early as possible. For this reason the script objectives given with the module objectives suggest a staggered introduction of hiragana and katakana, reflecting the distinctions between recognition, reading, limited reproduction, guided writing and free writing. As far as the timing of the introduction of katakana is concerned, teachers should be aware that introducing one script (for recognition) while learners are simultaneously learning another, also for recognition, *may* present problems and teachers may need to experiment to find the most suitable time for each group of learners.

Teachers should refer to the script objectives in the Stage A, Stage B and Stage 1 modules for examples of how the introduction of katakana could be approached.

Introducing kanji for recognition

Kanji for recognition is introduced in the same way as hiragana and katakana for recognition; that is, learners have opportunities to see and read kanji, but do not need to write kanji in order to complete an activity.

The 'kanji for recognition' included in the modules are suggestions only. They also indicate the kanji introduced in the resource materials which support the modules. Decisions about how many kanji should be introduced, and whether and how they should be assessed, are not addressed in these curriculum guidelines as these decisions are for schools, teachers and systems to determine.

It is generally believed that learners should be exposed to a variety of authentic and semi-authentic written material from an early stage. This will reduce the 'mystique' of written Japanese and, not least, develop valuable comprehension skills.

In introducing kanji for recognition teachers may wish to use some of the following strategies:

- Develop mnemonic explanations for frequently appearing kanji;
- Encourage learners to scan newspapers and magazines, etc., to find familiar words, sentences and numerals, e.g. dates;
- Cut out (where possible) and paste familiar kanji on a pin-up board;
- Use simple kanji when writing on the board, with or without furigana as appropriate.

Planning a unit of work

In selecting appropriate activities for a lesson or group of lessons, teachers need to apply a range of criteria such as 'complexity of the task', 'amount of preparation time required' and 'appeal to learners'.

The first section of this chapter explains some of the criteria applied by experienced teachers when making these decisions and organising their lessons. The second section focuses on how teachers might select the language to introduce for a series of activities. This is followed by brief sections which suggest exercises for introducing language for activities and factors to consider when selecting a particular strategy. The chapter concludes with an example of a step-by-step approach to developing a unit of work using these curriculum materials.

Activities

Selecting activities

A number of issues will influence teachers' decisions when selecting activities for a series of lessons. Following is a summary of these criteria which may assist teachers in planning and organising their lessons. Further information on this issue is presented in the *ALL Guidelines*, Book 2, pages 26–30.

Predictability
Activities in which language is predictable, e.g. where contextual clues assist learners to understand or be understood, are generally less demanding than activities where language is not as predictable.

However, given the importance of coping with unpredictability in language learning, it is important that learners are regularly exposed to appropriate amounts of language which is 'just beyond their reach'. This will help sharpen their guessing skills, their strategic skills (e.g. requesting clarification, repetition) and, not least, their comprehension. Too much unpredictability, of course, can reduce a learner's confidence or interest in an activity, and have a negative impact on language learning.

In order to provide learners with appropriate amounts of unpredictable language, teachers may wish to apply some of the following strategies:

- use pictures alongside written texts or together with spoken passages to provide contextual clues to support the meaning of the new or slightly unfamiliar language;
- provide simple English equivalents of key (unpredictable) language;
- allow learners more time than usual to complete an activity;
- encourage learners to work in pairs or small groups;
- encourage learners to focus on the more predictable language and less on the unpredictable language content.

Familiar and static
Learners generally find easier activities which:

- are based around topics and experiences which learners can relate to, or cultural experiences which they understand;
- focus on static or unchanging events such as a single picture or situation as opposed to more dynamic events such as a series of situations, e.g. a visit to a restaurant.

Level of support
Learners will generally find activities easier when they are able to:

- ask a partner, members of a group or their teacher for assistance rather than working individually;
- draw support from a sympathetic speaker, e.g. one who responds to the learner's lack of comprehension by repeating, using gestures or rephrasing with a simpler or more familiar question to re-establish the learner's confidence.

Level of processing
Learners generally find easier activities which:

- are grammatically simple;
- involve short rather than long pieces of text;
- do not contain too much unfamiliar language;
- involve clear spoken text delivered at a manageable speed;
- (in the case of written text) require learners to use recognition, reading or writing skills which are within their reach;
- follow a logical order of events or experiences.

Level of cognitive demand

The following scale of activities is adapted from the *ALL Guidelines*, Book 2, page 29, and indicates the type of activities with a low level of cognitive demand (1) to a high level of demand (7):

1. *memory*, e.g. activities where learners recall or recognise information and answer questions about specific details in the spoken or written text;
2. *translation*, e.g. activities where learners scan a piece of written or spoken text in order to identify a number of specific details;
3. *interpretation*, e.g. activities where learners take notes from a piece of spoken or written text and use the notes in some way;
4. *application*, e.g. activities where learners discuss and resolve a problem such as in a simple debate;
5. *analysis*, e.g. activities where learners think about and make choices from a number of given possibilities;
6. *synthesis*, e.g. activities where learners need to apply original or creative thinking;
7. *evaluation*, e.g. activities where learners give a spoken or written review or evaluation of something such as a skit, TV program or short talk.

Other factors

Learners will also generally find easier activities which:

- have few participants, e.g. one or two speakers rather than three or four;
- have few steps;
- provide opportunities to use acquired language rather than requiring understanding of a large percentage of new language.

In order to participate successfully in a sequence of activities, learners will need to be familiar with a range of language elements or language exponents, e.g. grammar and vocabulary. The following section discusses approaches to selecting and introducing this language to learners.

Selecting language for an activity

In the activities-based approach it is recommended that language is taught in the context of how the language may be used. This may mean, for example, teaching a verb tense, e.g. しました, teaching several items of vocabulary, e.g. やすみ, しゅうまつ, がっこうのあとで, and then considering how the structures may be combined

and used in a purposeful context. While this approach can be very effective, the task of continually finding new and interesting ways for learners to use acquired grammar and vocabulary can be extremely demanding for busy teachers.

An alternative approach is to consider the language activity which is to be the goal of the lesson (or lessons) and, *from the activity*, select the language learners will need to successfully complete the activity.

The steps below may assist teachers in applying this approach.

Steps for selecting language for an activity

Step 1

Select the activity (or activities) to be the goal of the lesson or lessons.

For example (from Stage 1, Module 4), '*Participating in an interview with a friend about leisure time, daily events and after-school activities.*'

Step 2

Determine what learners will be doing in the activity. The suggested activities in the modules typically represent this with words ending in 'ing'.

For example, *participating in an interview*.

Step 3

Consider the topics which learners will be communicating about, e.g. interviewing about. The suggested activities often contain examples of topics which may be useful in the activity.

For example, *leisure time, daily events*.

Step 4

Isolate useful language exponents suggested by Step 3. Refer to the Module Checklists for a range of suggested language exponents for each module.

For example, *participating in an interview about leisure time*, e.g.:
- しゅうまつに何をしますか。
- (かいものをし)ます。
- がっこうのあとで何をしますか。
- ときどき(テレビをみ)ます。

participating in an interview about daily events, e.g.:
- 何時に(おき)ますか。
- 6時はんに(おき)ます。
- それから何をしますか。
- たいていシャワーをあびます。

Step 5

Consider other language which may be useful (or required), e.g. to bring the activity to life, to maintain communication.

For example, *responding to interview questions and answers*, e.g.:

- それはいいですね。
- ああ、そうですか。

clarifying information, e.g.:

- ちょっとわかりません。
- もう一どいってください。

Exercises

Introducing and practising language for activities

As described in the chapter, 'The activities-based approach', classroom procedures or strategies which focus on language practice are referred to as exercises.

Listed below are some of the wide range of exercises commonly used by teachers when introducing language exponents or particular items of grammar and vocabulary.

- aural discrimination exercises
- filling-in-the-gap or cloze exercises
- matching parts of sentences
- inferring meaning of incomplete words
- crazy sentences
- sentence completion
- dictation
- spelling
- matching words or captions to pictures
- yes/no or true/false exercises
- multiple-choice exercises
- pattern practice
- aural comprehension
- word building
- vocabulary expansion exercises
- crosswords/word sleuths
- most word games
- jumbled words or sentences

Selecting exercises

A number of factors need to be considered when selecting exercises. Some are outlined below.

Listening and speaking first

It is generally accepted that exercises which focus on reading and/or writing skills are usually not effective unless learners have had sufficient practice in listening to and speaking the language beforehand.

Monitoring effectiveness

When using an exercise for the first time, teacher and learners will often find it less than perfect. After a 'new' exercise has been trialled in the classroom several times, it may be useful to discuss with learners how the exercise was or was not helpful and how it could be modified for future use.

Relevance to activity

Decisions about which exercise to employ can often be influenced by the type of activity for which the exercise is being practised. For example, if learners require language for a message-writing activity, an exercise which focuses on small message-like reading and writing tasks, e.g. listening to short sentences and writing one or two word summary 'messages', may be useful. Similarly, an activity focusing on 'telephone interaction' may be effectively practised by a listening and speaking exercise rather than one involving reading and/or writing.

To learn it, use it!

In some forms of exercises there can be a tendency to over-practise the language required before the exercise meaningfully commences. This can reduce the exercise to a task of providing 'obvious' or repetitive information, where little thought (and little learning) is taking place.

Exercises can be said to be most effective when:

- most learners are likely to make some errors (at least initially);
- there is an incentive not to make errors, e.g. to win a game;
- they require learners to perform some mental operation, e.g. select the answer from a group of alternatives or respond with a 'true' or 'false';
- the exercise takes place in a supportive atmosphere, e.g. learners are not criticised or punished if they make errors.

Accuracy or fluency?

While accuracy will be important in all exercises, in some exercises there will be a *focus* on accuracy, e.g. allowing learners plenty of time to answer a question and discuss or correct errors. In other forms of exercises there will be a *focus on fluency*, e.g. the speed with which learners can fill in the gaps in a guided dictation. Whether an exercise focuses more on accuracy or fluency will depend on the teaching and learning circumstances and what seems appropriate at the time.

A repertoire of exercises

While teachers (and learners) are likely to develop 'favourite' exercises, over-reliance on the same exercises can reduce their effectiveness. On the other hand, teachers may be tempted to discard 'tried-and-true' techniques in favour of newer exercises which might appear to offer attractive results. It may be advisable for less experienced teachers to introduce new exercises to their repertoire every so often, rather than all at once.

Developing a unit of work

Whereas the modules and module checklists present suggested objectives, activities, related learning experiences and language content, it is the teaching program which describes what will actually take place with a group of learners over a period of time. The program will serve as a record of what has been taught, what will be learned and how it will be assessed. In these curriculum guidelines, the teaching program is referred to as a *unit of work*.

The style, content and level of detail of a unit of work will depend heavily on the experience and circumstances of the teacher who will use it. The following information about developing a unit of work is, therefore, intended to be a suggested approach to programming, to be modified as required.

Below are a number of steps which teachers may wish to follow in developing a unit of work which integrates the components and approach in these curriculum guidelines.

Steps for developing a unit of work

Step 1
Select a module to be the starting point of the unit of work and familiarise yourself with the contents of the module and the module checklist. See:

- 'Sample learning pathways' (page 8);
- 'Stage 1 and Stage 2 target groups' (page 9);
- 'General objectives' (page 13)

for an indication of the broad scope of the module or stage selected.

Step 2
Select a unit of work title which suits the part of the module on which teaching and learning will focus. See:

- 'Suggested units of work' (page 18);
- the suggested units of work described in each module.

Step 3
Identify a number of module objectives to be achieved in the first unit of work. See:

- 'Module objectives' (page 16) for information on how the module objectives have been developed and how they relate to activities.

Step 4
Select the first activity to be the goal of the first or first few lessons. This activity should relate to one or more of the selected module objectives. See:

- 'Module objectives' (page 16) for information on how the module objectives can suggest particular activities. The diagram on page 34 also illustrates the relationship between module objectives and activities.
- 'Suggested activities' (page 16) for information on the types of activities described in the modules.

Step 5
Identify the language exponents or language elements, e.g. grammar and vocabulary, suggested by the first activity. See:

- 'Selecting language for an activity' (page 31).

Step 6
Select exercises (or strategies) for introducing or practising the language elements identified in Step 5. See:

- 'Introducing and practising language' (page 32);
- 'Selecting exercises' (page 32).

Step 7
Repeat Steps 4–6 for subsequent activities and exercises.

Step 8
Identify resources to be used for activities and exercises. See:

- 'Related resources' (page 123) for suggestions about suitable resources;
- resources developed for use with these curriculum guidelines.

Step 9
Identify activities which will be used for assessment. See:

- the chapter on assessment.

Step 10
Identify other learning experiences. See:

- 'Other learning experiences' (page 18);
- other learning experiences suggested in the modules.

Step 11
Evaluate the effectiveness of the unit of work, e.g. decide which aspects need to be modified for future use. See:

- 'Evaluation and curriculum renewal' in the *ALL Guidelines*, Book 4, pages 6–10.

Using module objectives to select activities

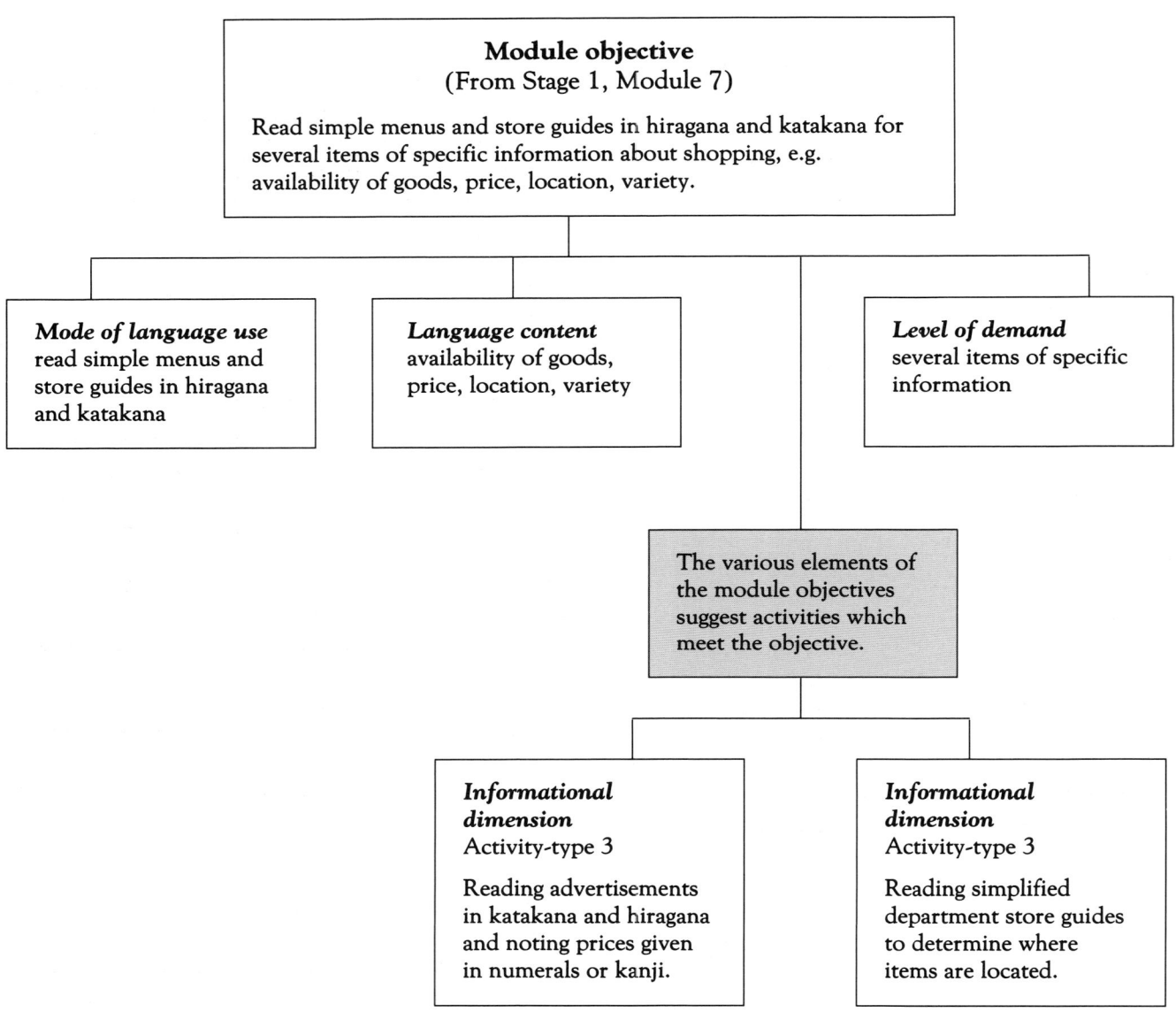

Module objective
(From Stage 1, Module 7)

Read simple menus and store guides in hiragana and katakana for several items of specific information about shopping, e.g. availability of goods, price, location, variety.

Mode of language use
read simple menus and store guides in hiragana and katakana

Language content
availability of goods, price, location, variety

Level of demand
several items of specific information

The various elements of the module objectives suggest activities which meet the objective.

Informational dimension
Activity-type 3

Reading advertisements in katakana and hiragana and noting prices given in numerals or kanji.

Informational dimension
Activity-type 3

Reading simplified department store guides to determine where items are located.

Assessment

The place of assessment

The process of assessment involves collecting information about learners' performance and making judgements about how satisfactorily they have achieved the objectives of the course. The objectives in these guidelines focus on what learners are *able to do* with their language knowledge and the focus of assessment is similar:

- what *modes of language use* learners are able to manage, e.g. a conversation, a caption, a letter;
- what *language elements* they are familiar with, e.g. どうやって学校へ行きますか。 たいてい、バスで行きます;
- the *level of expected performance*, e.g. a sentence of three or four words, a talk of about one or two minutes.

To ensure that assessment reflects what has actually been taught, considerations about objectives are an essential part of the assessment process. The following information therefore places assessment as *part of* the learning process and *not something added on* at the end of a series of lessons.

This chapter is intended to serve several purposes:

- to assist teachers in planning, selecting, describing and reporting on learner performance in assessment activities in a way consistent with how those activities were taught;
- to suggest an approach to assessment consistent with national LOTE initiatives, e.g. the *ALL Guidelines* and the *National Assessment Framework for Languages at Senior Secondary Level (NAFLaSSL)*;
- to provide assessment guidelines which can be applied with some flexibility to suit local school and accrediting requirements.

Purposes of assessment

There are many reasons why teachers conduct assessment. Among these are:

- to provide an additional purpose for learning;
- to find out what learners can do and how well they can perform, rather than simply reporting a numerical score;
- to understand learners better;

- to judge the effectiveness of a sequence of lessons;
- to give learners an understanding of the part they play in their own learning;
- to inform relevant people about learners' progress.

A number of assessment procedures can be employed to cover these purposes. However, some procedures are more effective for achieving particular purposes than others. It is therefore important to be clear about the purpose(s) of assessment *before* selecting an assessment procedure.

Assessment procedures in these curriculum guidelines serve two general purposes: *formative* and *summative*.

Formative assessment

Formative assessment is used to take a 'snapshot' of learners' progress during their course. It provides feedback for both teachers and learners, and answers the following types of questions.

For teachers
- How have learners progressed through a particular part of the course, e.g. over a number of lessons?
- What do I need to teach next (or again)?
- What specific information can I give learners about their recent progress?
- What aspects of the teaching process need to be reviewed or changed?

For learners
- How well have I performed over the last few lessons?
- How satisfactory is the work I have handed in?
- What do I need to do to improve my Japanese?

Summative assessment

The main purposes of summative assessment (end-of-term/semester/year) are to answer the following types of questions.

For parents
- What gains has my child made in learning Japanese?

For receiving institutions
- In what class or group should this learner be placed?

For teachers and other interested parties
- What level has this class reached?
- What level have individuals in this class reached?
- Is this group of learners progressing as well as last year's?
- How effective has my teaching program been?

Using module objectives to select assessment activities

Within each module, the selection of learning activities is governed by the module objectives. Similarly, in order that learners are assessed on what they have actually learnt, *assessment activities should also reflect the module objective(s) of a lesson or series of lessons.*

In order to decide which assessment activities will suit which module objectives, it can be helpful to focus on the sub-elements contained in each module objective:

- a *mode of language use*, e.g. give a talk, understand a sign, ask and answer questions;
- an *indication of language content*, e.g. a weekend outing, pets, after-school interests;
- an *indication of the level of expected performance*, e.g. a short (conversation) containing three to four items of well-rehearsed information.

These elements are illustrated in the diagram below which indicates how particular activities are suited to particular module objectives because they contain the same (or similar) elements.

As a means of assessing efficiently, it is often possible to select an activity which will meet a *combination of module objectives.* For example, during a conversation (*interpersonal dimension*) it may be possible for learners to provide small amounts of information about people and/or pets, etc. (*informational dimension*).

Module objective
(from Stage 1, Module 4)

Ask and answer several simple, well-rehearsed questions about free time, e.g. time, place, and make and respond to simple suggestions.

Mode of language use
Ask and answer questions

Language content
free time (e.g. time, place), simple suggestions

Level of demand
several simple, well-rehearsed (questions)

The various elements of the module objectives suggest assessment activities which meet the objective.

Interpersonal dimension
Activity-type 1

Making a short telephone call to discuss arrangements, e.g. to watch a video, go shopping, go on an outing.

Interpersonal dimension
Activity-type 1

Interviewing a friend about leisure time, daily events and after-school activities.

Formative assessment procedures

Formative assessment procedures can be used to assist in identifying learners' strengths and weaknesses at particular points in the course.

The following descriptions of methods of formative assessment may assist your selection of appropriate ways of finding out how learners are progressing. Examples of some of these methods are provided in the following pages, using pro formas (for photocopying) which can be found in the appendix, 'Assessment support materials'.

- *Observation checklists:* written checklists of items against which teachers check learners' achievement informally, e.g. by observing their conversation skills, their participation in activities, their performance in listening for understanding, the quality of their pairwork. (See samples on pages 38 and 39; pro formas on pages 135 and 136.) Similar lists can be used by learners for self or peer assessment (see below).
- *Spot tests:* short (5 to 10 minute) tests which focus on particular language exponents, grammar or vocabulary.

- *Oral work records:* appraisals of pieces of learners' spoken work (e.g. recorded on audio tape), using criteria such as those suggested in the sample assessment form on page 44. (Pro forma on page 140.)
- *Written work records:* appraisals of pieces of learners' written work, using criteria such as those suggested in the sample assessment form on page 45. (Pro forma on page 141.)
- *Peer and self assessment:* learners provide feedback to each other or assess their own performance in an activity. (Samples on pages 42 and 43; pro formas on pages 137, 138 and 139.)
- *Progress cards:* learners check their progress (e.g. with one or more objectives, activities or language exponents), firstly by themselves and, later, by peers and/or the teacher. (Sample on page 43; pro formas on pages 137 and 138.)
- *Progress logs:* learners (or the teacher) keep a record of specific progress, e.g. a list of the books or magazines learners have read, the activities they have completed.
- *Anecdotal records:* written records based on observation of day-to-day performance and/or discussion with learners.

Sample: General objectives teacher checklist
(end of Stage 1)

The items listed here are taken from the Stage 1 general objectives on page 13. Teachers would not normally use all the items shown. A pro forma is provided on page 135.

General objectives checklist

Name _Betty Pryor_   Class _8A_   Date _20 Nov._

~~I can~~ _Betty_ can: seldom   always

- follow short spoken classroom instructions

- use everyday expressions, e.g. greetings

- introduce self

- ask and answer short, well-rehearsed questions about topics covered in this unit

- engage in and sustain a short conversation about a familiar theme

- develop and present short role-plays and skits

- write short letters and journals

- listen to short spoken presentations to extract specific items of information

- listen to short spoken presentations and write short lists

- listen to short spoken presentations and extract the overall gist

- give short spoken presentations about familiar topics

Sample: Learning skills teacher checklist
(end of/during Stage 1)

The items listed here are adapted from the *ALL Guidelines*, Book 2, pages 55–58. Other suggestions can be found in *Stages B–D of a K–12 Series of Syllabus Exemplars: Italian*, pages 63–65. A pro forma is provided on page 136.

Learning skills checklist

Name ___Betty Pryor___ Class __8A__ Date ___14 July___

~~I can~~/ ___Betty___ can:

	seldom	always
• participate independently and cooperatively in groups and class activities		
• share information with others		
• take risks		
• use strategies to assist learning, e.g. mnemonic devices		
• meet work targets, e.g. completion of activities, homework		
• understand ~~his~~/her part in own learning		
• evaluate ~~his~~/her own learning		
• understand sociocultural aspects of the language ~~he~~/she has learnt		
• understand and use Japanese script(s)		
• pronounce Japanese clearly and accurately		
• convey meaning in speech accurately		

Sample: Peer assessment of general objectives (end of Stage 1)

The items listed here are taken from the Stage 1 general objectives on page 13. Teachers would not normally use all the items shown. A pro forma is provided on page 135.

General objectives checklist

Name _Tony Castello_   Class _8A_   Date _28 Nov._

~~I can~~ / _Tony_ can: seldom   always

- understand instructions (in Japanese) given by the teacher
- use everyday expressions, e.g. greetings
- introduce self
- ask and answer questions about the topics covered
- have a conversation with someone in the class
- take part in role-plays and skits
- write letters and personal journals
- listen to Japanese speakers and get the gist of what they are talking about
- give a short talk about the topics covered
- listen to Japanese speakers and understand the information they are giving
- read hiragana and katakana and understand what is being written about

---

Sample: Self-assessment of learning skills
(end of/during Stage 1)

The items listed here are adapted from the *ALL Guidelines*, Book 2, pages 55–58. Other suggestions can be found in *Stages B–D of a K–12 Series of Syllabus Exemplars: Italian*, pages 63–65. A pro forma is provided on page 136.

Learning skills checklist

Name _Maria Konstantinidis_   Class _8A_   Date _30 June_

I can/_____ can:	seldom ———————— always
• work by myself and work in a group	always
• share information with others	(mid)
• have a go when not quite sure	(mid)
• use hints given by my teacher and my textbook for learning Japanese	(high)
• get my work done	always
• do things to help me learn better	(high)
• look at what I'm doing and say how well I'm progressing with Japanese	(high)
• understand why people often bow when they talk to each other	always
• understand hiragana and katakana words	(high)
• pronounce my Japanese clearly	(mid)
• say what I want to say in Japanese using the sentences we have learnt	(mid)

Sample: Self-assessment
(across Stages 1 and 2)

The items listed here are taken from the *ALL Guidelines*, Book 2, page 53. A pro forma is provided on page 137.

Self-assessment form

Name _Peter Dean_   Class _9B_   Date _4 May_

Activity: *I had to imagine that I was someone else, interview a partner and then introduce her to the class.*

What I have achieved:
I asked Melissa lots of questions in Japanese and she understood me. I was surprised that I was able to stand up and introduce Melissa as Madonna and talk about her in Japanese — I thought I'd be really nervous and forget what she'd told me. I also thought that I'd probably laugh as Melissa doesn't look like Madonna but everyone was really serious.

Difficulties I encountered:
I found it hard at first to decide who to be but then I thought I'd be Elton John and borrowed Jason's funny round glasses. I interviewed Melissa who was pretending to be Madonna. I found it hard to remember what she told me and I couldn't remember how to say 'say that again' in Japanese. Also because Madonna doesn't go to school, I couldn't ask some of the things I'd worked out.

Strategies for improvement:
Next time I think that I'll work out more questions. Also I'll find out how to say 'say it again' and 'hold on, I need to write that down.' I probably also should practise katakana more so that I can write faster.

Sample: Self/peer/teacher assessment of progress
(Stage 1, Module 4, *Free time*)

The items listed here are adapted from the Stage 1, Module 4 module objectives. Teachers may wish to modify the items, e.g. include more or other examples. A pro forma is provided on page 138.

<table>
<tr><th colspan="4">Progress card</th></tr>
<tr><td>Name <u>Sue Mitchell</u></td><td colspan="3">Class <u>8A</u></td></tr>
<tr><td></td><td>Checked by me</td><td>Checked by a partner</td><td>Checked by my teacher</td></tr>
<tr><td><s>I can/</s> <u>Sue</u> can:</td><td>Date</td><td></td><td></td></tr>
<tr><td>• listen to a short spoken passage for 4 or 5 items of information such as:
– the time
– the day
– after-school activities
– how people travel to and from school</td><td>_____ ☐</td><td>14 Sept. ☑</td><td>_____ ☐</td></tr>
<tr><td>• give a short talk giving 5 or 6 items of information about free time such as:
– what I do on the weekends
– what I do after school
– when I play sport
– when I go to my friend's house
– my free time interests</td><td>_____ ☐</td><td>20 Sept. ☑</td><td>_____ ☐</td></tr>
<tr><td>• find 4 or 5 items of information written in a letter in hiragana such as:
– what the people do on weekends
– how they get to school
– things they like and dislike</td><td>_____ ☐</td><td>20 Sept. ☑</td><td>_____ ☐</td></tr>
<tr><td>• write short lists in hiragana, e.g. things to do with a friend on the weekend</td><td>_____ ☐</td><td>30 Sept. ☑</td><td>_____ ☐</td></tr>
<tr><td>• write a short caption for a poster about free time</td><td>_____ ☐</td><td>30 Sept. ☑</td><td>_____ ☐</td></tr>
</table>

Sample: Judging performance in listening and speaking
(Stage 1, Module 4, *Free time*)

The boxes for the criteria selected for assessing performance in the particular activity have been filled in. A pro forma is provided on page 140. Other criteria for judging performance could be added as appropriate (some may be more applicable to Stage 2):

- relevance and appropriateness of response;
- breadth of treatment of topic;
- organisation and development of topic;

- degree of interest, imagination or creativity;
- knowledge of subject matter.

Listening and speaking

Name _Tony Castello_ Class _8A_ Date _14 Sept._

Activity _Participating in an interview with a friend about leisure time, daily events and after-school activities._

もっと
がんばりましょう

たいへん
よくできました

Receptive (listening)

■ level of support required to understand, e.g. prompting, repetition

■ degree to which learner understood important details of what was said

☐ degree to which learner understood the gist of what was said

■ degree to which learner coped with unpredictability, e.g. change in topic, unfamiliar words

Productive (speaking)

■ accuracy of what was said, e.g. grammar, vocabulary

■ intelligibility of pronunciation

☐ socio-cultural appropriateness of what was said

■ range and variety of language used

☐ degree to which learner attempted to go beyond their very familiar language range

☐ degree to which learner used strategies to sustain communication

☐ degree to which learner's speech 'flowed', e.g. within sentences, between sentences

☐

☐

☐

☐

This page may be photocopied for student/teacher use only. © Curriculum Corporation 1993.

Moshi Moshi Teachers' Handbook

Sample: Judging performance in reading and writing
(Stage 1, Module 4, *Free time*)

The boxes for the criteria selected for assessing performance in the particular activity have been filled in. A pro forma is provided on page 141.

Reading and writing

Name _Maria Konstantinidis_   Class _8A_   Date _14 Sept._

Activity _Writing a summary of the weekend's activities, using abbreviated sentences or single words, e.g. to represent the days, times, events._

	もっと がんばりましょう	たいへん よくできました
Receptive (reading)		
☐ level of support required to understand the written information		
☐ degree to which learner understood important details of what was written		
☐ degree to which learner understood the gist of what was written		
☐ degree to which learner coped with unpredictable or unfamiliar written words		
Productive (writing)		
■ accuracy of what was written, e.g. grammar, vocabulary	ⓘ	
■ socio-cultural appropriateness of what was written		ⓘ
■ range and variety of language and script used		ⓘ
■ degree to which learner attempted to go beyond their very familiar language range	ⓘ	
☐ degree to which learner's writing 'flowed', e.g. within sentences, between sentences		
☐		
☐		
☐		
☐		
☐		
☐		

Summative assessment procedures

Summative assessment is used to provide a picture of learners' overall achievement in a course. It is generally carried out in the following situations:

- at the end of a Stage, e.g. to determine whether learners are ready to proceed from one Stage to the next;
- at the end of a module or group of modules;
- at the end of a term, semester or year.

Summative assessment can be administered as an examination if the system requires it, or as a series of procedures involving carefully-chosen, controlled activities, e.g. spread over several class sessions.

As the main purpose of summative assessment is to provide as clear a picture as possible of learners' overall performance, it is important that summative assessment procedures *represent but do not replicate* the range of activities learners have been taught, e.g. in a module, a Stage or a semester. This can be achieved by ensuring that the summative assessment procedures reflect the range of module objectives covered in the Stage or the point at which learners are being assessed.

Deciding on weightings

While these curriculum guidelines do not suggest an 'ideal' weighting for assessment procedures, it is important that, as a general principle, the balance of activities for assessment reflects the general balance of learning activities in the course. It is important that the aggregation of scores over several assessment activities or procedures also reflects this balance.

Sample summative assessment procedures

Sample end-of-Stage summative assessment procedures are provided below. However, teachers should note the following:

- The samples are intended as a guide only. The range of language content covered in the samples is likely to vary from school to school, from system to system and from State to State.
- The samples represent a cross-section of the module objectives contained in each Stage. It is not possible for a series of summative assessment procedures to cover every module objective and every activity which learners have covered.

- In some schools or systems it will not be feasible to implement end-of-Stage assessment procedures. It may be necessary to use end-of-term/semester/year procedures, in which case the range of modules represented in the following samples would not apply.

At the end of this chapter is a step-by-step guide which may assist teachers in developing their own assessment procedures.

End of Stage 1
Conversation

1. Learners take part in an interview with their teacher on topics they have covered in the term/semester/year, e.g. self, family, friends, interests. Some questions could be based on pictures or photos which the teacher supplies or the learner brings to the interview, e.g. a family album.
   (Interpersonal: listening/speaking)
2. In small groups or with their teacher, learners respond to cue cards in a simple role-play, e.g. requesting a number of items in a shop, asking about the items on a menu. Learners are assessed individually.
   (Interpersonal: listening/speaking)

Prepared talk

Learners select a topic of interest from a number of alternatives supplied by their teacher and deliver a short, prepared talk. The talk should include a number of linking devices, e.g. そして, でも, それから and cover several prescribed sub-topic areas.
(Informational: speaking)

Listening for information

Learners listen to a simple conversation in a familiar setting and identify several items of information, e.g. listening to a conversation in a post-office and noting the cost and number of stamps requested, the destination of the letter.
(Informational: listening and writing)

Reading for information

Learners read a letter from a Japanese friend about a forthcoming visit and write a summary of their main questions about what to do, what the weather will be like, when are the best times to visit, and write a list of the possibilities to answer each question.
(Informational: reading and writing)

Written expression

Learners write a short piece to promote something, e.g. an item in a shop, a restaurant they would like to visit, a sport they play.
(*Aesthetic: writing*)

Weightings

The following approximate weightings are considered appropriate for end-of-Stage 1 assessment procedures such as those outlined above:

Conversation	45%
Prepared talk	15%
Listening for information	15%
Reading for information	15%
Written expression	10%

End of Stage 2

The examples below are intended as a guide only and reflect only a cross-section of the module objectives covered in Stage 2. As before, in some States and systems these sample procedures may be more appropriate in an end-of-term/semester/year context.

Conversation

Learners take part in a conversation with their teacher for 5–10 minutes on a range of topics they have covered, e.g. their own interests, other people, holidays, how they spend their money. During the conversation there should be several changes of topic.
(*Interpersonal: listening/speaking*)

Problem-solving role-play

Learners take part in a simple role-play (with a small group of other learners or their teacher) in which they are required to solve a simple problem or negotiate some difficulty, e.g. finding how to get to several places in a town, department store or school, explaining to a homestay guest where particular items can be found in the home.
(*Interpersonal: speaking/listening*)

Prepared talk

Learners give a short talk on a prepared topic giving a range of factual details, descriptive information and simple reasons. The talk may focus on one or more photos or pictures selected by the learner.
(*Informational: speaking*)

Listening for information

Learners listen to a variety of spoken texts (e.g. simple announcements, conversation between shopkeeper and customer) and extract the overall gist and/or several items of specific information. Learners will use the information for tasks which might include completing a chart, making a short summary (in English or Japanese as appropriate), marking true or false, matching to pictures.
(*Informational: listening and writing*)

Reading for information

1. Learners read a short letter and write a brief reply, e.g. answering the person's questions, making suggestions, giving simple instructions.
    (*Informational: reading and writing*)

2. Learners read a variety of simple signs, brochures, maps or menus and use the information they contain for tasks which might include making simple summaries (in English or Japanese as appropriate), completing tables, matching to pictures or photos, marking the route on a map.
    Informational: reading and writing)

Written expression

1. Learners write 50–60 characters on a topic they have covered, e.g. My holiday, My best friend, Last weekend.
    (*Informational/Aesthetic: writing*)

2. Learners write a series of connected sentences as a personal response to a photo or picture, e.g. of a holiday attraction, an exciting or peaceful scene, an interesting or unusual person.
    (*Aesthetic: writing*)

Weightings

The following approximate weightings are considered appropriate for end-of-Stage 2 assessment procedures such as those outlined above:

Conversation	30%
Problem-solving role-play	10%
Prepared talk	15%
Listening for information	15%
Reading for information	15%
Written expression	15%

Developing summative assessment procedures

Step 1
Select the module objectives on which the assessment is to be based. These could be drawn directly from particular modules or a summary of a group of module objectives.

Teacher checklist:
- Is the number of module objectives selected realistic?
- Are the three dimensions of language use (interpersonal, informational and aesthetic) and the skills of listening, speaking, reading and writing represented?

Step 2
Determine the weightings for the dimensions, e.g. interpersonal 40%, informational 40%, aesthetic 20%. Refer to the section 'Deciding on weightings' on page 46.

Teacher checklist:
- Do the weightings reflect the amount of time spent on or emphasis given to particular dimensions during the term or semester?

Step 3
Identify suitable activities which will meet the objectives. Refer to the chart 'Using module objectives to select assessment activities' on page 36.

Teacher checklist:
- Will learners be doing something which is evidence of language learning, e.g. not just paper folding or mask making?
- Will the activities allow individual learners' ability to be judged independently? (The quality of one learner's part in a role-play activity may be dependent on the quality of other learners' input.)
- Are the activities fair to the learners, e.g. do the skills, level of demand and language content reflect what learners have actually learnt?
- Will learners encounter some unpredictability and not just repeat well-rehearsed 'lines'?
- Do the activities cater for the range of learners' abilities?
- Will learners be able to show their true ability or are the activities likely to show 'one off' performance?

Step 4
Select criteria for judging performance in each activity (or group of activities). Refer to the pro formas on pages 140 and 141.

Teacher checklist:
- Are the criteria realistic for learners at this stage of their course, e.g. is the level of demand in the activities 'too easy' or 'too hard'?
- Do the criteria match the demands of the activities?
- Do the criteria take account of the fact that learners' skills (listening, speaking, reading and writing) will not all be developed to the same extent? (Receptive skills — listening and reading — will usually be better developed than productive skills — speaking and writing.)
- Are background speaker standards being applied to learners where these are not appropriate?

Step 5
Decide how learners' performance will be measured or graded, e.g. allocation of an alphabetical grade A, B, C or D, allocation of a number score to the various criteria identified from the pro formas on pages 140 and 141.

Teacher checklist:
- Is the grading scheme (the allocation of marks or grades to learners' performance) manageable and realistic?
- Has the grading scheme been trialled on a group of learners and modified where necessary?
- Is there more emphasis on how many errors learners make than on how much meaning they get across?

Step 6
Reflect on and modify the assessment scheme where this is feasible and manageable.

Teacher checklist:
- Can learners perform the activities in the given time?
- Do the activities discriminate between learners?
- Do the criteria chosen accurately reflect the characteristics of learners' performance in the activity?
- Are there particular features, e.g. errors or confusing instructions, in one or more of the activities, which stand in the way of learners performing to capacity?
- Are there redundant activities, e.g. those which give little or no extra information about learners' performance?

Stage 1
Modules

Module titles and suggested units of work

Module	Suggested units of work
1 How do you do? よろしく	• Pleased to meet you • All about us • First steps with Japanese script
2 Family and friends かぞくとともだち	• About me • Family and friends • Pets
3 Things about me じぶんのこと	• I like... • School • Sport
4 Free time フリータイム	• After school • My weekend • Making a video
5 Neighbourhoods きんじょ	• Home • My neighbourhood • Maps and signs
6 The four seasons 四季（しき）	• Seasonal activities • Weather and weather forecasts • The seasons in Japan
7 Welcome いらっしゃいませ	• Shopping • Advertising • Restaurant visit
8 Media マスコミ	• Newspapers and magazines • TV guides • Japanese TV shows

Symbols appearing with some of the listed activities indicate that accompanying resources are provided in the Teachers' Resources (▢) or the Student Book (✪).

How do you do?
よろしく

Stage 1　Module 1

Module objectives

Learners should be able to:
- follow short, very explicit spoken instructions, requiring short verbal or physical responses, e.g. classroom management;
- listen to short personal introductions for several items of personal information, e.g. name, age, place of residence, telephone number;
- greet people at school using high frequency learned patterns and responses;
- introduce themselves and other learners, giving several items of well-rehearsed personal information, e.g. name, nationality, telephone number;
- ask and answer several simple, well-rehearsed questions about themselves and other learners, e.g. place of residence, age, nationality;
- read familiar words in hiragana for simple pieces of written information, e.g. a person's age, simple greetings;

Script objectives
- recognise *some* familiar words in hiragana;
- recognise and write own name in katakana.

Other learning experiences

(may be conducted in English)
- On a map of the world, marking the countries from which class members or their family have emigrated and discussing languages used.
- Discussing the Japanese hiragana syllabry.
- Practising dictionary skills, e.g.:
  - finding the page in a dictionary on which a particular word is located;
  - finding the word listed before or after a given word.
- Practising reading skills, e.g.:
  - reading signs, e.g. of classroom objects and instructions placed around the room;
  - grouping signs in categories, e.g. those with particular hiragana combinations.

Suggested units of work

- Pleased to meet you
- All about us
- First steps with Japanese script

Suggested activities

Interpersonal

Activity-type 1
Interacting and discussing

はなこさん、
こんにちは
In small groups, exchanging personal information, e.g. greetings, name, age, address, telephone number. ❏

Introducing self to other learners, teachers, visitors and bowing appropriately.

しゅっせきです
Responding to roll call and following simple classroom instructions. ❏

Giving information about a learner; others guess the identity, e.g. age, address, nationality.

Playing 'せんせい Says' (as for 'Simon Says').

あなたのなまえは？
Using Japanese names, introducing self to class, memorising as others speak, then seeing how many people can be identified. ✪

はじめまして！
Using a new identity, exchanging information, e.g. name, age, address. ✪

Role-play
Introducing a character to the class, e.g. using puppets.

Role-play
Greeting, introducing and farewelling people around the school, e.g. meeting the principal, greeting friends and teachers.

Activity-type 2
Interacting to get things done

Script
Making a class duty roster on which learners write their own names in katakana.

Informational		Aesthetic	
Activity-type 3 Getting information and using it	**Activity-type 4** Giving information	**Activity-type 5** Making a personal response	**Activity-type 6** Personal expression

Activity-type 3
Getting information and using it

みなさんきいて
ください！

Listening to classroom commands and matching to pictures. ❑

じこしょうかい

Listening to じこしょうかい and completing details on a chart, e.g. name, age, nationality, residence. ❑

どこからきましたか

Reading short written profiles of people who live in Japan, finding where they live and matching the people to the appropriate place on a map. ❑

Activity-type 4
Giving information

Script
Making name tags in katakana.

Recording じこしょうかい to be sent to a sister school, neighbouring school or other Japanese class.

Script
Assigning own name in katakana to portraits.

Activity-type 5
Making a personal response

Using characters from Japanese *manga*, giving personal introductions.

Activity-type 6
Personal expression

Creating a design or page border using hiragana and/or katakana characters.

Rearranging segments of personalities cut out from magazines into unusual 'people' and introducing these to the class.

Colouring or filling in an outline of own name in katakana with pictures which reflect personality.

Module checklist

Key functions and notions	Suggested language exponents
Greeting others	おはようございます。 （メリーさん）、おげんきですか。 はい、げんきです。
Leavetaking	さようなら。 バイバイ。 じゃ、また。
Using modes of address	（　）さん （　）くん （　）せんせい （　）ちゃん
Introducing self and others	はじめまして。（メリー）です。どうぞよろしく。 こちらは（トム）さんです。ともだちです。
Asking for and giving information about:	
● name	おなまえはなんですか。 わたしは（メリー）です。 ぼくは（さぶろう）です。
● age	なんさいですか。 （　）さいです。
● year of schooling	なんねんせいですか。 （　）ねんせいです。
● place of residence	どこにすんでいますか。 （アリス・スプリングス）にすんでいます。
● nationality	どこからきましたか。 （ニュージーランド）からきました。 （オーストラリア）人です。
● telephone number	でんわばんごうはなんばんですか。 （400–2143）です。
Asking for reciprocal information	（　）さんは？ （　）くんは？
Asking for and giving confirmation	（12さい）ですか。 はい、そうです。 いいえ、（13さいです）。
Responding:	
● to class roll call	（　）さん！ （　）くん！ はい！ （メリーさん）はけっせきです。
● to apology/thanks	どういたしまして。

How do you do? よろしく

Key functions and notions	Suggested language exponents
Following classroom instructions	みなさん、（すわっ）てください。 （ほんをあけ）てください。 （きいて）！
Apologising	すみません。 ごめんなさい。 おそくなってすみません。
Attracting attention	すみません。
Asking for repetition	もういちどいってください。
Expressing lack of comprehension	わかりません。
Asking for clarification	(pointing)　にほんごでなんですか。 「にっき」です。
Expressing gratitude	ありがとう。 どうもありがとうございます。

Suggested kanji for recognition

一、二、三、四、五、六、七、八、九、十、人

Family and friends
かぞくとともだち

Stage 1 　 Module 2

Module objectives

Learners should be able to:

- listen to short talks and conversations for several simple items of information about friends and family, e.g. family members, age, month of birth, pets;
- ask and answer several simple, well-rehearsed questions about friends and family;
- give a short spoken presentation about self, friends and family, involving manipulation of a range of well-rehearsed sentences;
- present a short role-play or skit with 2 or 3 participants, involving manipulation of familiar sentences about friends and family, e.g. hobbies, pets;
- read several short familiar sentences (in hiragana) for simple information about friends and family;

Script objectives
- recognise *all* hiragana;
- write *some* familiar words in hiragana, including own name in katakana. (See Module 1.)

Other learning experiences
(may be conducted in English)

- Discussing how the hiragana and katakana scripts evolved and how they are currently used.
- Creating a class mural of family pets in origami.
- Comparing and contrasting family life in Japan and Australia and other countries relevant to learners.
- Researching origins of Japanese and English names and comparing.
- Researching the meaning of pet names and choosing one.

Suggested units of work

- About me
- Family and friends
- Pets

Suggested activities

Interpersonal

Activity-type 1
Interacting and discussing

Who would I like to be?
Selecting a new identity, e.g. name, age, residence, nationality, brothers and sisters, then introducing self to other learners. ✪

Role-play
Meeting friends or other families and 'catching up', e.g. introducing a family guest, talking about pets, congratulating someone on their birthday.

Asking class members about things they do with family and friends, and completing a grid.

Finding out about other learners' families by asking questions, e.g. about brothers and sisters.

Activity-type 2
Interacting to get things done

ペットをかっていますか？

In groups, exchanging information about pets and deciding which are popular. ❏

Informational		**Aesthetic**	

Activity-type 3
Getting information and using it

かぞくのはなし
Listening to simple information about families, e.g. parents, number of children, pets, and matching to pictures. ❑

ペットはどこでしょう？
Listening to owners giving short descriptions of their pets, e.g. type, size, and matching to pictures. ❑

さぶろうさんのかぞく
Listening to information about family members and completing a chart, e.g. name, age, month of birthday, Chinese birth sign. ❑

おもしろいともだち、
おもしろいかぞく
Reading simple accounts of places people visit with family and friends, and deciding whom they would most like to meet. ✪

Looking at simple Japanese family cartoons, e.g. サザエさん and discussing what might be happening.

Activity-type 4
Giving information

十二し
Making a 十二し (Chinese animal birth sign chart) and recording family details, e.g. names, birth months, ages, under the appropriate animal sign. ✪

じこしょうかい
Giving a short guided talk about self in the role of another character. ✪

Script
Making a family album with photos and simple information in hiragana, e.g. captions, short sentences, a family tree, pets.

Script
Placing cut-outs on sheets of places learners visit with family and friends, and labelling with appropriate words and phrases.

Activity-type 5
Making a personal response

Singing songs related to family and friends e.g. 「十人のインディアン」

Role-play
Using pictures, magazine cut-outs or photos of animals, neighbours introduce their 'new pets' to each other.

Activity-type 6
Personal expression

たんじょうびカード
Writing a simple message for a birthday card. ❑

Skit
Introducing a pet to the other animals at 'Obedience school'.

Module checklist

Key functions and notions	**Suggested language exponents**

Asking and giving information about:

● family

（　）さんはなん人かぞくですか。
かぞくはなん人ですか。
（四）人かぞくです。
（四）人です。
（ちちと）…と私です。
（おかあさん）の名前はなんですか。
（はは）の名前は（　）です。
（　）（ちゃん）は（小さい）です。

● age

（　）さんはなんさいですか。
（　）さいです。

● month of birth

（　）さんのたんじょうびはなん月ですか。
（三）月です。
（私）のたんじょうびは（三）月です。

● Chinese birth sign

（　）さんはなにどしですか。
（へび）どしです。

● pets

ペットをかっていますか。
ペットは？
はい、（犬）を（一）ぴきかっています。
いいえ。

（ペット）の名前はなんですか。
「（くろ）」です。

（犬）は（大きい）ですか。
はい、（大きい）です。
いいえ、（小さい）です。

● hobbies

しゅみはなんですか。
あなたのしゅみはなんですか。
（ビデオ）です。
わたしのしゅみは（スポーツ）です。

● ownership

これはだれのですか。
（　）さん／わたしのです。

● places to go with family and friends

（かぞく／ともだち）とどこにいきますか。
（レストラン）にいきます。

（えいが）にいきますか。
ええ、いきます。
いいえ、いきません。

Asking about and identifying objects

これはなんですか。
（にっき）です。

Expressing approval

いいですね。
それはいいですね。

Family and friends かぞくとともだち

Key functions and notions	Suggested language exponents
Expressing surprise	へえ！ あれ！ ああ、そうですか。
Exclaiming	かわいい！
Congratulating	（おたんじょうび）おめでとう。 おめでとうございます。

Suggested kanji for recognition

大、小、名前、月、私、犬

Things about me
じぶんのこと

Stage 1   Module 3

Module objectives

Learners should be able to:
- listen to short talks and conversations for several items of simple information about likes and dislikes, e.g. foods, sports and school subjects;
- ask and answer several simple, well-rehearsed questions about likes and dislikes, e.g. school subjects;
- give a short spoken presentation involving several well-rehearsed items of simple descriptive information about likes, dislikes and school subjects;
- present a short role-play involving manipulation of several familiar sentence patterns, e.g. a dinner table conversation, a simple school scene;
- read a short letter (in hiragana) for several items of specific information about likes, dislikes and simple descriptions;

Script objectives
- write short sentences in hiragana.

Other learning experiences
(may be conducted in English)
- Visiting a Japanese restaurant or food shop.
- Making an origami chopstick holder.
- Preparing a Japanese meal in the classroom.

Suggested units of work
- I like . . .
- School
- Sport

Suggested activities

Interpersonal

Activity-type 1
Interacting and discussing

Compiling simple questions about likes and dislikes in food and drink, and interviewing.

かるた
Script: Playing food and drink *karuta*. ❏

好きですか？
Asking people about likes and dislikes (school subjects) and recording the information on a chart. ❏

Pairwork
Writing a list of school subjects and sports, then asking a friend questions about them, e.g. びじゅつをべんきょうしていますか。好きですか。フランス語は？テニスは？テニスが好きですか。

'Life. Be In It' survey
Asking friends about sports they play and the types of foods and drinks they consume. ❏

Role-play
Presenting a dinner table scene, e.g. a conversation about school, favourite foods.

Activity-type 2
Interacting to get things done

好きなメニュー
Planning simple menus for special occasions, e.g. birthdays and restaurant visits, and writing them on menu cards. ✪

'Food mind games'
Selecting a food or drink and writing clues, e.g. category (くだものです), colour (きいろいです), description (あまいです), then trying to guess the item (selected by a class member) based on the clues given.

Informational		**Aesthetic**	

Activity-type 3
Getting information and using it

いちごも好きです
Listening to short conversations and identifying the things people like to eat and drink. ❏

がっこうのかもく
Listening to conversations about school subjects and finding out which are the most popular. ❏

なにをたべますか？
Reading a simple menu from a Japanese restaurant and discussing what to eat and drink with a friend. ✪

Reading short accounts of the subjects people study, their likes, dislikes and favourites, and trying to identify the learner who suits the information given.

せいかくテスト！
Reading the alternatives in a 'personality' quiz, selecting those which apply, working out the total individual score and reading the given personality profile. ✪

Activity-type 4
Giving information

Giving a short talk comparing Japanese and Australian meals.

Script
Writing a number of sentences to accompany a picture or photograph of a favourite food, sport or school subject.

さあ、レストランへ！
Making a classroom poster advertising a Japanese restaurant. ✪

Giving a short talk on school subjects, e.g. which are studied, likes, teachers.

Activity-type 5
Making a personal response

Activity-type 6
Personal expression

Designing a 'Healthy Foods' poster.

Script
Writing shape poems about favourite foods.

Performing a short skit depicting a meal time, e.g. at home, at a friend's house, on a school camp.

Drawing a promotional poster for a school subject or school activity.

Module checklist

Key functions and notions	Suggested language exponents

Enquiring about and expressing likes and dislikes

（きゅうり）が好きですか。
はい、好きです。
はい、だい好きです。
まあまあです。
あまり好きじゃないです。
いいえ、好きじゃないです。
いいえ、好きではありません。
いいえ、好きじゃありません。
いいえ、きらいです。
いいえ、だいきらいです。

じゃ、（かぼちゃ）は？
（私）は（かぼちゃ）が（好き）です。

あなたは？
（私）も（テニス）が好きです。

どんな（スポーツ）が（好き）ですか。
（テニス）が（好き）です。
（すいえい）も（好き）です。

Asking and giving information about:
● descriptions

（コーヒー）は（おいしい）ですか。
はい、（おいしい）です。
いいえ、（まずい）です。
（コーヒー）は（おいしい）です。
（テニス）はどうですか。
（おもしろい）です。
（テニス）はだめです。

● school subjects and sports

（びじゅつ）をべんきょうしていますか。
はい、べんきょうしています。
いいえ、べんきょうしていません。

どんな（スポーツ）をしていますか。
（テニス）をしています。

Requesting something

（みかん）をください。
（みかん）と（アイスクリーム）をください。

Offering something

（みかん）です。どうぞ。
（やきとり）をどうぞ。
どうぞ、（たべ）てください。

Things about me じぶんのこと

Key functions and notions	Suggested language exponents

Suggested kanji for recognition

好き、日本語

Free time
フリータイム

Stage 1   Module 4

Module objectives

Learners should be able to:
- listen to a short spoken passage for several items of simple information about free time e.g. days, times, simple events;
- ask and answer several simple, well-rehearsed questions about free time (e.g. time, place) and make and respond to simple suggestions;
- give a short talk involving several well-rehearsed items of simple descriptive information with simple links, about free time and free time activities;
- find several items of simple information in a short letter (written in hiragana) about free time, e.g. days, places, times;
- write short lists in hiragana, e.g. things to do with a friend during the weekend;
- write a short caption for a poster or picture about free time;

Script objectives
- use hiragana for all written tasks.

Other learning experiences
(may be conducted in English)
- Discussing travelling to school in Japan, e.g. long distances for some students, means of travel, じゅく, late return home.
- Discussing しゅうがくりょこう, e.g. who goes, how often, mode of travel (bus, しんかんせん), おべんとう.
- Discussing popular holiday destinations in Japan, e.g. Kyoto, Nara, Hokkaido, Kyushu.
- Discussing daily routine and free time activities for Japanese students, e.g. visiting デパート、はんかがい.

Suggested units of work
- After school
- My weekend
- Making a video

Suggested activities

Interpersonal

Activity-type 1
Interacting and discussing

Making a short telephone call to discuss arrangements, e.g. to watch a video with a friend, go shopping, go on an outing.

'20 Clues'
Guessing the mystery place given clues, e.g. かぞくと行きます。コーラをのみます。ゲームをみます。ときどきゲームをします。たのしいです。どこですか？

Participating in an interview with a friend about leisure time, daily events and after-school activities.

いつかいものに
行きますか？
Asking and answering questions about shopping routines, e.g. who shops where and when, what people typically buy, and recording the information on a chart. ❑

メッセージ
Writing a message to a friend suggesting a weekend or after-school activity. ✪

アンケート：
ウィークエンド
Asking what people did on the weekend, filling in a chart and finding the popular activities. ❑

Activity-type 2
Interacting to get things done

Drawing scenes of weekend activities and describing the scene to a partner who draws the information.

Planning an ideal weekend or rainy day and writing the activities on a schedule.

いつ行きましょう？
Making arrangements with a partner for a suitable time and day for a leisure activity, and writing a summary of the main details. ✪

Planning what to do with a Japanese visitor and writing a short list of the likely activities, including days and times.

Informational

Activity-type 3
Getting information and using it

どうでしたか？
Listening to passages about free-time activities and completing a paragraph. ❏

じゅんばんに！
Looking at pictures depicting free time activities and arranging pictures in sequence according to spoken descriptions. ❏

何をしているのでしょう？
Reading short accounts of how people spend their weekend and drawing a simple illustration to suit the information. ✪

けんじくんからのてがみ
Reading a short letter about a weekend activity (e.g. places visited, what people did, what things were like, likes and dislikes) and discussing the letter with a friend. ✪

Activity-type 4
Giving information

Making a list of items needed for a weekend, e.g. at a beach house, school camp, school or family outing.

Giving a short talk, e.g. about a favourite leisure activity, holiday outing.

Keeping a simple journal recording free time activities, e.g. times, what things were like.

ちょうさ：ひまなじかん
Completing a questionnaire about leisure activities. ❏

Making a class collection of photographs of learners involved in leisure activities and writing captions and labels.

Writing a summary of the weekend's activities, using abbreviated sentences or single words to represent, e.g. the days, times, events.

Writing a list of the things learners do after school.

Script
Writing a simple, short report after a class visit to a restaurant, e.g. what people had to eat and drink, what the meal was like and who went.

Aesthetic

Activity-type 5
Making a personal response

Singing popular Japanese songs, e.g. children's songs, simple folk songs.

Writing personal captions to picture stories.

どうですか？
Looking at stimulus pictures depicting leisure activities in Japan and writing responses, e.g. I like . . . , I am going to . . . , Let's . . . , etc. ✪

Looking at videos depicting Japanese learners making a poster depicting scenes from the video and writing captions.

Activity-type 6
Personal expression

まんが
Filling in speech balloons in cartoons depicting leisure activities. ❏

Designing a 'Life. Be In It' poster with an interesting caption.

Making a video 'A day in our lives', depicting learners talking (or presenting skits) about their daily life and/or weekend activities and sending to a sister school or nearby school where Japanese is studied.

Module checklist

Key functions and notions	Suggested language exponents

Asking and giving information about:
- time

いま、何じですか。
(10)じ(はん)です。

何じに(テレビ)を(み)ますか。
(5)じ(はん)に(み)ます。

- day

(きょう)は何曜日ですか。
(月曜日)です。

いつ(かいもの)に(行き)ますか。
(土曜日)に(行き)ます。

(金曜日)に(パーティー)に(行き)ますか。
はい、(行き)ます。
いいえ、(行き)ません。

- place

(どこ)で(かいもの)を(し)ますか。
(スーパー)で(し)ます。

- after-school activities

がっこうのあとで何を(し)ますか。
(ともだち)の(うち)に行きます。
そのあとで何を(し)ますか。

(きのう)がっこうのあとで何を(し)ましたか。
(ともだちのうち)に行きました。

- transport

どうやって(がっこう)に(き)ますか。
(じてんしゃ)で(き)ます。

- frequency

まいにち、(バス)で(き)ます。
ときどき、あるいて(き)ます。

よく、スポーツをしますか。
ええ、よく(し)ます。

Making and responding to suggestions

(日曜日)に何を(し)ましょうか。
(えいが)を(み)ましょう。
ええ、(み)ましょう。
いいえ、(ビデオをみ)ましょう。

じゃ、そうしましょう。

いつ(み)ましょうか。
(土曜日)に(み)ましょう。

Stating opinions

(クリケット)は(おもしろい)です。
(これ)は(まずい)です。
(キャンプ)は(たのしかった)です。

Free time フリータイム

Key functions and notions	Suggested language exponents
Disagreeing	いいえ、（おいしい）です。 いいえ、（つまらなかった）です。
Emphasising opinions	（おいしい）ですよ。 （たのしかった）ですよ。 そうですよ。
Identifying self and requesting someone (over the telephone)	もし、もし、（〜）ですが。 （〜）さんおねがいします。 はい、おまちください。

Suggested kanji for recognition

日曜日、月、火、水、木、金、土、何、行く

Neighbourhoods
きんじょ

Stage 1　Module 5

Module objectives

Learners should be able to:

- listen to short spoken passages for several items of simple information about the neighbourhood, e.g. home, favourite places, location;
- give a short talk with supporting photos or pictures providing several items of descriptive information about the local area, e.g. places of interest, location;
- engage in and sustain a simple conversation about the neighbourhood;
- identify specific items of information from simple Japanese neighbourhood signs, e.g. opening and closing times, アイスクリームや;
- write short summaries of information on a neighbourhood theme, e.g. the main rooms in a house, favourite places in a neighbourhood;
- write a short creative passage giving several pieces of information about an ideal or imagined place, e.g. a new house, an ideal neighbourhood;

Script objectives
- recognise *some* familiar words in katakana.

Other learning experiences
(may be conducted in English)

- Discussing photos and pictures of Japanese homes.
- Using pictures, discussing Japanese 'neighbourhoods', e.g. streets, amenities, shops, schools, vending machines.

Suggested units of work

- Home
- My neighbourhood
- Maps and signs

Suggested activities

Interpersonal

Activity-type 1
Interacting and discussing

Asking and answering questions about neighbours, e.g. number in family, what they are like, what they do on weekends or in the evenings, if you like them.

好きなところ
Asking friends about places in the local area, which attractions they like and dislike and completing a survey sheet. ❑

Interviewing each other to find the popular places in the neighbourhood and marking them on a local map.

Asking a friend about the electrical items they have at home and noting their responses.

Activity-type 2
Interacting to get things done

Role-play
Telephoning:
- a friend and arranging a visit, e.g. asking what time they will finish homework or sports practice, suggesting a place and time for an outing;
- a parent, saying where you want to go and what you want to do and answering their questions, e.g. about day, time, transport.

Group work
'Good Neighbours': Deciding on the criteria for determining whether people are 'good neighbours', e.g. what the family and their pets are like, how often/when they have parties, and writing a group summary.

Complete the maps
Asking and answering questions with a partner to fill in details of places on a neighbourhood map. ❑

Informational

Activity-type 3
Getting information and using it

From a list in katakana, of class members, writing lists which group learners in various ways, e.g. who live close by, travel on the same bus, belong to particular clubs or groups.

まちのちず
Listening to spoken clues, labelling an incomplete map of a neighbourhood, including buildings, shops, schools, friends' houses, own house and leisure attractions. ❏

4LDK です
Listening to descriptions of Japanese houses and matching to floor plans. ✪

ローラーブレードで行く！
Listening to dialogues about where people are going and selecting pictures to match the place, the transport and the time. ❏

キムさんのインタビュー
Listening to an interview about day-to-day topics and selecting the responses given. ❏

Activity-type 4
Giving information

私の家
● Drawing a floor plan of own house and a room in the house, and labelling the rooms and room contents in Japanese. ✪

Making Japanese signs for display in the classroom or use around the school.

Mapping out a walk around the school neighbourhood, e.g. drawing and labelling places, writing simple captions about places of interest, places to avoid.

Showing a number of photos or drawings about the neighbourhood and giving a short talk to other learners.

Showing a photo or picture of own house and describing some of the features shown, e.g. the main rooms, the garden.

Writing a summary list, e.g.:
● of places in the neighbourhood learners like to visit;
● of favourite shops;
● of most treasured possessions.

Aesthetic

Activity-type 5
Making a personal response

Looking at pictures or photos of places of interest to learners and writing a simple personal response, e.g. describing what is liked or disliked about the place, describing own impressions of things in the picture.

Using stimulus pictures, comparing neighbourhoods in Australia and Japan.

Activity-type 6
Personal expression

私のドリームハウス
Writing a paragraph about an ideal house and labelling a picture. ✪

すごい！
Creating an advertisement, e.g. for a house, a school, a shop, suburb or town. ✪

Module checklist

<table>
<tr><td>Key functions and notions</td><td>Suggested language exponents</td></tr>
</table>

Asking for and giving information about:

● neighbourhood places

(家)の(となり)に(何)がありますか。
(スーパー)や(レストラン)や(こうえん)があります。

● places in and around the home

あなたの(家)に(何)がありますか。
(プール)や(にわ)があります。

(プール)がありますか。
ええ、あります。
いいえ、ありません。

● location

(アイスクリームショップ)はどこですか。
(えき)の(前)です。

● what a place is like

(シドニー)はどんな(まち)ですか。
(大きい)(まち)です。

(あなた)の(へや)は(大きい)ですか。
ええ、(大き)いです。
いいえ、(大き)くないです。

● duration
  – of years

どのぐらい(ホーバート)にすんでいますか。
(1)ねんぐらいすんでいます。
(10)ねんすんでいます。

  – of clock time

(学校)は何時から何時までですか。
(8)時(はん)から(3)時(はん)までです。

● favourites

一ばん好きな(ところ)はどこですか。
(こうえん)です。

● degree

(こうえん)は(大きい)ですか。
ええ、とても(大きい)です。
いいえ、ちょっと(小さい)です。

(それ)は(ちょっと)(へん)です。

Asking for and giving opinions

(すうがく)はどうですか。
(やさし)いです。
(やさし)くないです。
(ちょっと)(へん)です。
(すごい)！
(いや)！

Neighbourhoods きんじょ

Key functions and notions	Suggested language exponents

Suggested kanji for recognition

前、何時、中、家、学校、書く、先生

The four seasons
四季(しき)

Stage 1   Module 6

Module objectives

Learners should be able to:

- listen to short spoken passages for several items of simple information about the seasons, e.g. the weather, favourite seasons, seasonal activities;
- give a short talk with supporting photos or pictures about the seasons, e.g. duration, weather, reasons for liking a particular season or holiday;
- engage in and sustain a simple conversation about the seasons and the weather, e.g. to make arrangements for an outdoor activity;
- read simple short letters, notes and messages containing familiar katakana words for specific information, e.g. about people, seasons, weather, activities, dates;
- write a short poem or imaginative account about the seasons or a seasonal activity, e.g. a hot day at the beach;
- write a short letter or journal entry, e.g. about a weekend or holiday activity;

Script objectives
- read *all* familiar words in katakana;
- write *some* familiar words in katakana.

Other learning experiences
(may be conducted in English)

- Listening to a recorded telephone weather report.
- Talking about seasonal events and celebrations, e.g. はなみ、おぼん.
- Writing *haiku* about the weather and seasons, in English.

Suggested units of work

- Seasonal activities
- Weather and weather forecasts
- The seasons in Japan

Suggested activities

Interpersonal

Activity-type 1
Interacting and discussing

ひま：ゆかりさんの一年
Asking and answering questions about seasonal leisure pursuits in Australia and Japan, e.g. when people go to the beach, go camping, look at さくら and もみじ. ✪

そちらのお天気は？
Writing a letter to a friend, beginning with comments and questions about the weather. ✪

Group work: giving a round-Australia weather report while other members of the group try to memorise the details.

お正月(しょうがつ)
Reading accounts of how Saburo and Yukari spent New Year and comparing with learners' own experiences. ✪

Activity-type 2
Interacting to get things done

あめなら...
Deciding on suitable activities to coincide with various weather conditions. ✪

Talking about the seasons, e.g. which are liked, which is favourite and why, what the weather is like in particular seasons.

Role-play
Telephoning a partner, asking what the weather will be like and arranging something to do.

どこに行きましょう？
Given a list of places and weather forecasts, deciding where to go to do a list of preferred activities. ❑

Activity-type 3
Getting information and using it

Listening to simple weather forecasts and:
- selecting appropriate pictures, e.g. things to do, what to take;
- writing a note to a friend about weekend plans;
- plotting temperatures on a graph;
- matching place names (in katakana) to pictures depicting the weather.

私も夏が好き！
Reading a letter (e.g. from a Japanese pen friend, containing information about the seasons, weather, likes, favourites) and comparing it to own preferences. ✪

Watching a video of a Japanese weather forecast and discussing it in English.

にっき
Reading a series of diary entries and sequencing the events. ❏

天気よほう
Listening to weather reports and completing the details in a chart. ❏

せかいの天気
Listening to a world weather forecast and noting the details in a chart. ❏

Activity-type 4
Giving information

Completing the daily information board, noting the day, date and weather.

Presenting a short weather forecast for a given place in Japan.

Using pictures depicting one or more seasons, writing about:
- seasonal activities in Australia and/or Japan;
- seasonal likes and dislikes, e.g. foods, drinks, sports, weekend activities.

そうですね。いやですね。
Presenting short dialogues about the weather. ✪

Activity-type 5
Making a personal response

しゃしん
Selecting a photo or picture which depicts an interesting aspect of the weather, e.g. an ocean storm, a hot day at the beach, and writing a brief response to the picture.

Listening to a song about the seasons, e.g. 「春が来た。」and drawing and labelling a picture in response.

Activity-type 6
Personal expression

Writing a paragraph about a favourite season or a poem about a favourite seasonal food, drink or activity.

はいく
Writing a short, simple poem, or *haiku* about the seasons and feelings about the seasons. ✪

'Never-ending story'
Creating an imaginary story about a Japanese and/or Australian family: each learner adds a line about the family.

Module checklist

Key functions and notions	Suggested language exponents

Asking for and giving information about:

● a particular season

（日本）では、（夏）は何月ですか。
（日本）では、（夏）は（六）月から（八）月までです。
（夏）は（何月）から（何月）までですか。

（いま）、（日本）で、きせつは何ですか。
（夏）です。

● date

（きょう）は（何日）ですか。
（十一月二十三日）です。

（こどもの日）はいつですか。
（五月五日）です。

（夏休み）は（いつ）から（いつ）までですか。
（十二月十四日）から（一月三十一日）までです。

● the weather
　– now

きょうのお天気はどうですか。
いいお天気です。
でも、ちょっとさむいです。
（あめ）がふっています。
くもっています。

（日本）は、もう（さむ）いですか。
ええ、もう（さむ）いです。
いいえ、まだ（さむ）くないです。

きおんは何どですか。
（21）どです。

　– from a weather forecast

（あした）のお天気はどうでしょうか。
（あめ）でしょう。
（さむい）でしょう。

● seasonal activities

（夏休み）に（何をし）ますか。
（うみへ行き）ます。

日本人は（春）に（何をし）ますか。
（はなみに行き）ます。

● favourites, likes and dislikes

一ばん好きな（きせつ）はいつですか。
（秋）です。

どのきせつが（好き）ですか。
（秋）が（好き）です。

Giving information about purpose

（ともだちのうち）へ（あそび）に行きます。
（こうえん）へ（さんぽ）に行きました。

The four seasons 四季（しき）

Key functions and notions	Suggested language exponents
Enquiring about and expressing reasons	なぜ好きですか。 （あたたかい）からです。
Asking about and expressing desire	（冬休み）に（何をし）たいですか。 （りょこうをし）たいです。 （しゅくだいをし）たくないです。

Suggested kanji for recognition

春、夏、秋、冬、天気、休み、年

Welcome
いらっしゃいませ

Stage 1　Module 7

Module objectives

Learners should be able to:

- listen to short spoken passages and simple announcements about shopping, for gist and specific details, e.g. item(s) being promoted, cost;
- engage in and sustain a simple conversation about shopping, e.g. shopping routines, permission, preferences;
- present a short role-play about a shopping visit with several participants, involving manipulation of a variety of patterns with simple substitutions and links;
- read simple menus and store guides in hiragana and katakana for several items of specific information, e.g. availability of goods, price, location, variety;
- write a short passage to promote something, e.g. a product, a shop;
- write lists and summaries containing a range of items, e.g. a menu, a list of items carried by a shop;

Script objectives
- Read *some* simple, unfamiliar words in katakana;
- write familiar words in katakana.

Other learning experiences

(may be conducted in English)

- Comparing shops, shopping streets, shopping centres and department stores in Australia and Japan.
- Keeping a collection of authentic material such as labels and packets of Japanese products, e.g. a scrapbook, ongoing pin-up board display.
- Writing about a Japanese shopping street, e.g. what shops are there, when they open and close, where the street is located.

Suggested units of work

- Shopping
- Advertising
- Restaurant visit

Suggested activities

Interpersonal

Activity-type 1
Interacting and discussing

Playing 'I went shopping and I bought...'.

Consumer Survey
Finding out the learners' contribution to the economy by adding the total amount spent by the class in a week. ❏

Playing　しんけいすいじゃく　(Concentration) with cards depicting products and product advertisements. ❏

これどう？
Using pictures of shops and things to buy in Japan, performing a short dialogue.

メモ：かいもの
Writing a memo of things to buy on a shopping visit. ❏

Activity-type 2
Interacting to get things done

Role-play
Telephoning someone and making arrangements to go shopping, e.g. when, how, what the weather might be like, what they want to buy.

Role-play
Comparing prices of goods at two shops to see which shop is the cheaper.

レストランへのけいかく
Organising what a party group will have at a Japanese restaurant by reading the menu beforehand. ✪

Role-play: Salesperson of the Year!
Acting out a scene where a salesperson is trying to impress, e.g. a customer, the shop owner, another salesperson.

Role-play
Persuading a customer why they should (or should not) buy a particular item.

Informational

Activity-type 3
Getting information and using it

Reading restaurant advertisements to find out what type of food is offered, opening and closing times, etc.

あちこちみせへ
Listening to short talks about shopping visits for specific information, e.g. purchases, quantity, cost, and completing a chart. ❏

何にしますか？
Listening to a restaurant conversation and finding out what people have ordered. ❏

何をたべる？
Listening to a dialogue and finding out what people are going to eat and how it's made. ✪

あんないじょ
Reading simplified department store guides to determine where items are located. ❏

さぶろうとゆかり
Reading short passages about Saburo and Yukari, and drawing pictures to suit the given information. ✪

Activity-type 4
Giving information

まちのサイン
Creating signs and notices in Japanese and displaying. ✪

Writing shopping lists for various occasions, e.g. a weekend camp, a video night, a party.

Writing a short passage promoting a local shopping centre, e.g. where it is located, what the shops are called, what they are like, why it is good to shop there.

Making a party shopping list based on what is needed and what is already in the house. ❏

ねだんは？
Reading advertisements and noting prices. ✪

Aesthetic

Activity-type 5
Making a personal response

Writing short advertisements to promote something, e.g.:
- a favourite food or drink;
- a Japanese food, drink or product;
- a restaurant or shop.

Activity-type 6
Personal expression

Developing and presenting a promotion for a new shop or product, e.g. an advertising jingle, an advertisement, a skit. The presentation could be recorded on video and shown to other classes or sent to a sister school or twin school.

Module checklist

Key functions and notions	Suggested language exponents
Asking and giving information about:	
● availability	すみません、（チョコレート）がありますか。 ええ、あります。 いいえ、ありません。 ありますよ。
● price	いくらですか。 （みかん）はいくらですか。 ぜんぶでいくらですか。 （一万二千五百）円です。
● location	（アイスクリームショップ）はどこにありますか。 （えき）の（前）にあります。 （みぎ）にあります。
Asking for, giving and withholding simple permission	（かいものに行っ）てもいいですか。 ええ、いいです。 ええ、（行っ）てもいいです。 いいえ、だめです。
Making and responding to suggestions about:	
● place	（日曜日）に（どこに行き）ましょうか。 （かいものに行き）ましょう。
● means	（何）で（行き）ましょうか。 （でんしゃ）で（行き）ましょう。
● people	（だれ）と（行き）ましょうか。 （はなこさんとジョンくん）と（行き）ましょう。
Interacting in a shop	すみません。 ごめんください！ いらっしゃいませ。 またどうぞ。 まいどありがとうございます。 かしこまりました。
Offering something	はい、どうぞ。 はい、（みかん）です。どうぞ。
Apologising (for keeping a customer waiting)	おまたせしました。
Asking about and identifying a particular item	どれですか。 どちらですか。 （どれ）が（やすい）ですか。 （これ）が（やすい）ですよ。

Welcome いらっしゃいませ

Key functions and notions	**Suggested language exponents**

Asking about and making simple requests

（アイスクリーム）をください。
（これ）と（これ）をください。
（チョコレートアイスクリーム）にします。

（デザート）は（何）がいいですか。
（いちご）がいいです。

Asking about and requesting quantities

いくつですか。
（コーラ）を（三本）ください。
（みかん、一つ）と（チョコレートを二まい）ください。

Suggested kanji for recognition

入口、出口、円、百

Media
マスコミ

Stage 1 Module 8

Module objectives

Learners should be able to:

- listen to short spoken passages for several items of specific information about media and media programs, e.g. preferences, times, descriptions;
- listen to a variety of simple spoken sources for overall gist, e.g. the product being promoted in an advertisement;
- participate with several others in a short role-play with a media theme, e.g. items of factual information;
- give a short talk about a media program, providing factual information, impressions, and several simple explanations, e.g. why the program is liked or disliked;
- read simplified TV guides for several items of specific information, e.g. program, program type, time, characters;
- write a short passage in hiragana and katakana giving factual information and simple opinions, e.g. about a media program, a media performer.

Other learning experiences
(may be conducted in English)

- Setting up a カラオケ party, e.g. at lunchtime.
- Watching a sub-titled Japanese movie or TV drama.
- Researching names of sub-titled Japanese movies available at local video rental shops.
- Researching and presenting a 'Did you know . . . ?' media feature on contemporary Japanese life, e.g. using sources such as airline magazines, English versions of Japanese newspapers and journals.

Suggested units of work

- Newspapers and magazines
- TV guides
- Japanese TV shows

Suggested activities

Interpersonal

Activity-type 1
Interacting and discussing

From a list of TV program categories, asking a partner which ones they watch. ❏

Role-play
Interviewing a TV or radio identity, e.g. asking which programs they watch, which are their favourites and why, when they watch TV.

Playing 「まるとばつ」 : Identifying true or false statements about TV programs, e.g. time, channel, identities, description.

Surveying class members to find out the most watched or listened to media programs and compiling a weekly ratings guide.

Talking about Australian and Japanese TV programs, e.g. which programs are popular, times, channels — NHK, TBS, ABC.

Giving spoken clues about a program (e.g. type, time, channel, personalities) from which others guess the name of the program.

Activity-type 2
Interacting to get things done

Pair work
Using a weekend TV guide, deciding which programs to watch.

Pair work
Using a simple rating scale, asking a partner to rate a number of TV programs, recording their responses and comparing with others.

Role-play
Asking a parent, e.g. to watch a late night TV program, buy a second TV for the house, watch a video.

何を見ましょう?
With a partner, deciding which TV programs to watch and writing the details on a memo. ❏

Exchanging information with a partner about free time schedules (including TV viewing) in order to arrange a date and place for a party.

Informational

Activity-type 3
Getting information and using it

テレビ番組
Listening to Japanese students discussing TV programs and summarising the information in a chart. ❏

せかいはせまい
Reading modified tour brochures and summarising the main details. ✪

ラジオたいそう
Following a leader giving directions for simple exercises. ✪

Listening to and watching Japanese TV commercials for information, e.g. the gist of the commercial, key words, familiar words, prices.

テレビガイド
Reading a TV guide and writing a summary (in English) of the programs learners can identify. ✪

Watching an episode of a Japanese TV drama and listing words and expressions which are identified.

Watching Japanese TV commercials and discussing what they might be about.

Activity-type 4
Giving information

Using cut-outs from local media magazines, making a TV guide, e.g. containing descriptions of TV programs, program types (i.e. えいが、ホームドラマ、まんが) time, channel, who is in the program, why it is (or is not) worth watching.

Writing simple reviews of TV programs.

Collecting pictures of media stars and writing about them.

Presenting a short written (or spoken) review of the week's best or worst program.

Presenting a short spoken account of a recent TV or video program, e.g. what it was about, when it was shown, what it was like, why the person liked or disliked it.

Preparing and presenting a 'top 10' music report.

Aesthetic

Activity-type 5
Making a personal response

Listening to popular music from Japan.

Creating a 'media corner' containing photos and pictures with captions, e.g. featuring weekly themes.

Activity-type 6
Personal expression

Writing a 'gossip column' featuring members of the class.

Presenting a 'Top 10' countdown.

Performing an unusual commercial, e.g. using the dress-up box, presenting a commercial where the actions or props do not match the script.

In a group, presenting a radio or TV segment, e.g. a news report, a weather report, music, interviews, commercials.

Writing an advertisement for a favourite program.

Module checklist

Key functions and notions	**Suggested language exponents**

Asking and giving information about:
- categories of likes and dislikes, e.g. programs

どんな（テレビばんぐみ）が（好き）ですか。
（コメディー）が（好き）です。

- particular likes and dislikes

どの（まんが）が（好き）ですか。
（トムとジェリー）が（一ばん好き）です。

- viewing habits

（ビデオ）をかりに行きますか。
ええ、（よく）かりに行きます。
いいえ、かりに行きません。

- when something happens

この（まんが）はいつやっていますか。
この（ホームドラマ）は何曜日にやっていますか。
（土曜日の7時はん）からです。

- where something is shown

何チャンネルでやっていますか。
（5）チャンネルでやっています。

- being allowed (or not allowed) to do something

まいにち（テレビ）を（見）てもいいですか。
ええ、（まいにち）（見）てもいいです。
いいえ、だめです。
（月曜日）から（木曜日）まで（見）てはだめです。

Understanding instructions

もう（しょくじ）ですよ。（テレビ）を（けし）てください。
（テレビ）をけして！

Understanding commands

けしなさい。

Enquiring about and expressing reasons for liking or disliking

なぜ（あのえいが）が（好き）ですか。
（おもしろい）からです。
（へんだ）からです。

Media マスコミ

Key functions and notions	Suggested language exponents

Suggested kanji for recognition

新聞、見る、聞く

Stage 2
Modules

Module titles and suggested units of work

Module	Suggested units of work
1 People 人々	• That's the story of my life! • People who interest me
2 24 Hours 二十四時間	• Weather forecasts • Journal entries and letter writing • A day in the life of 田中さん
3 Around the school 学校あんない	• My school day • A school in Japan • School information brochure
4 Money もらったお金で	• Part-time jobs • Clothing and fashion • Shopping in Japan
5 Holidays 休暇（きゅうか）	• Planning a holiday • Holiday journal • A holiday in Japan
6 Homestay in Australia 日本からのお客様	• Before the homestay guest arrives • In and around my house • My homestay guest
7 Variety show バラエティーショー	• Developing the variety show • Putting on the show
8 What happened this year 今年のでき事	• This year at school • Our magazine • The best thing for me this year was . . .

Symbols appearing with some of the listed activities indicate that accompanying resources are provided in the Teachers' Resources (▢) or the Student Book (◉).

People
人々

Stage 2　Module 1

Module objectives

Learners should be able to:

- listen to extended spoken texts for specific personal information, e.g. about physical characteristics, traits and capabilities;
- listen to a piece of descriptive information about someone and summarise what is heard;
- engage in and sustain a short conversation about people, e.g. interests, physical characteristics, capabilities, future career;
- give a short talk about someone, e.g. their background, schooling, capabilities and interests;
- read descriptive accounts of people and their interests, and summarise the information presented;
- write a personal profile, e.g. including personal and physical characteristics, interests, achievements, career and/or schooling;
- write a personal response to a picture or photo of someone, e.g. describing the person as if they were a friend.

Other learning experiences
(may be conducted in English)

Looking at videos, e.g. 'The human face of Japan' and 'Faces of Japan', discussing aspects such as the personalities, lifestyles of participants and noting similarities and differences between Japan and Australia.

Suggested units of work

- That's the story of my life!
- People who interest me

Suggested activities

Interpersonal

Activity-type 1
Interacting and discussing

いいともだち
In groups, ranking the qualities of an ideal partner, e.g. physical appearance, capabilities, and comparing to select the most interesting. ❏

Writing a complimentary message about another learner and giving it to them or sticking it to their back.

Role-play
Using the 'dress-up box', meeting someone, e.g. at a party, and comparing likes, dislikes and interests.

パーティーであった
Pair work: Describing someone met at a party while a partner selects from a set of pictures. ✪

Deciding on new identities, (e.g. name, characteristics, age, schooling, interests), exchanging information about each other, then introducing each other to the class.

Group work
Writing names on a sheet and passing to a neighbour who writes a sentence about the person indicated. The sheets are passed on simultaneously, after each comment, until they reach the person the comments refer to. Class discusses the comments.

Activity-type 2
Interacting to get things done

デート
Using cue cards, arranging a blind date over the telephone. Learners describe themselves and ask and answer questions to organise their date, e.g. where to meet, where to go and what to do. ❏

Pair work
Giving details about the identity of a suspect (from notes or cue cards) while partner tries to identify the suspect from among a set of pictures.

Role-play
Interviewing a 'new student' (e.g. about their personal background, interests, capabilities), and suggesting a club or activity they may like to join.

Informational		**Aesthetic**	

Informational

Activity-type 3
Getting information and using it

まいご
Listening to 'missing child' announcements and deciding which picture or photo matches the description. ✪

Writing and reading out cards containing information about learners while others try to guess their identity, e.g. せがたかいです。　めがあおくないです。

Listening to or reading descriptions of teachers' personalities and trying to guess their identity.

スクール・レポーター
Listening to じこしょうかい and writing short summaries (using words, partial or complete sentences) for the school magazine. ❑

おもしろい人ですね
Listening to 'gossip' about people and writing summaries of what is said. ✪

Activity-type 4
Giving information

Writing and presenting a personal history of self or other person of interest.

Recording class talks and presentations on video and keeping to show learners in their final year of Japanese or sending to students in sister school.

Writing notes or summaries about the characters in a favourite TV program or movie.

Aesthetic

Activity-type 5
Making a personal response

Watching a segment from the 「ヤンさんと日本の人々」 video series and writing a paragraph about one of the characters.

Writing a description about a person from a photo or magazine cutout.

へんじをかきましょう
Writing a reply to a letter in a magazine. ✪

Activity-type 6
Personal expression

Cutting out the speech bubbles from cartoons and writing own dialogues, e.g. questions and comments about other people.

Writing a paragraph describing self with a different identity.

Module checklist

| Key functions and notions | Suggested language exponents |

Asking for and giving information about:

● physical characteristics

（　）さんはどんな人ですか。
（せが高い）です。
（あしがなが）くて（目が茶色）です。

● zodiac/Chinese birth sign

（　）さんのせいざは何ですか。
（やぎざ）です。
（私）は（さるどし）で（おひつじざ）です。

● character traits

（しんせつ）です。
（しんせつ）で（おもしろい）人です。

● clothing and other details

めがねをかけています。
たいてい、赤いネクタイをしています。
（あおいぼうしをかぶって）います。

● personal interests

（　）さんはどんな事が好きですか。
（ダンスをする）事が好きです。

（私の）しゅみは（本をよむ事）です。

● capabilities

（テニス）ができますか。
（スキーをする）事ができますか。
はい、できます。でも、あまり（上手）じゃないです。
いいえ、ぜんぜんできません。

（トムくん）は（ピアノ）が（ほんとうに上手）です。

● birth, birth place

生年月日はいつですか。
（77）年（8）月（21）日です。

何年に生まれましたか。
（千九百七十七）年に生まれました。

● duration

どのぐらい（日本語）を（べんきょうし）ていますか。
（二年はん）（べんきょうし）ています。

● future career

（何）になりたいですか。
（パイロット）になりたいです。

People 人々

Key functions and notions	Suggested language exponents

Suggested kanji for recognition

口、耳、高い、茶色、黒、赤、青、上手、下手、事、年、生

24 hours
二十四時間

Stage 2　Module 2

Module objectives

Learners should be able to:
- listen to a variety of spoken texts for specific information, e.g. a weather forecast, a recorded message;
- engage in and sustain a short conversation about daily life and routines, e.g. free time, arrangements to meet someone, asking permission;
- present a short spoken account of the day's highlights, e.g. events, feelings, what things were like;
- develop and present a short role-play with several participants, featuring a daily life situation, e.g. meeting friends after school;
- read descriptive accounts of daily experiences and events, e.g. from a journal or letter, and write a brief note or message in response;
- write short journal entries about daily life and routines.

Other learning experiences
(may be conducted in English)

Discussing similarities and differences between Australian and Japanese teenagers' daily lives.

Suggested units of work
- Weather forecasts
- Journal entries and letter writing
- A day in the life of 田中さん

Suggested activities

Interpersonal

Activity-type 1
Interacting and discussing

田中花子さんは何時におきますか
Using *Japan Foundation Slide Bank*: 生活シリーズ, exchanging information about aspects of daily life in Japan, e.g. transport to school or work, meals, shopping.

天気は？
Asking and answering questions about the weather each day. ❑

Role-play
Telephoning parents to ask permission to go on an outing, stay at a friend's house or come home late. ✪

学校は？
Role-play: Telephoning a friend who was absent from school and talking about the day's events. ✪

In small groups, writing then reading diary entries to each other, e.g. about the weather, daily activities, impressions.

Role-play
Questioning people on the street about their daily lifestyle, e.g. for a shopping centre or magazine survey.

Activity-type 2
Interacting to get things done

Ranking the Top 7
- Listing the most likely things parents ask learners to do each day. ✪
- Listing the most likely responses from parents after asking for permission to go out at night or stay at a friend's house.
- Listing the most frequently complained about topics by learners.

Using the entertainment pages from newspapers, making arrangements to see a movie, go to a concert or other special event.

Role-play
- You are watching a good movie on TV, but it's late and a parent wants you to go to bed. What will you say to the parent to let you continue watching?
- Your child stays up late watching TV whenever he or she wants to. What will you say to convince your child to go to bed in order to be wide awake for the next school day?

まず...それから...
Pair work: Sequencing a series of events by asking and answering questions with a partner. ❑

Informational		Aesthetic	

Informational

Activity-type 3
Getting information and using it

にっき
Looking at a journal entry with parts missing and writing suggestions for the missing details. ❑

ちがいますよ!
Using *Japan Foundation Slide Bank*: 生活シリーズ identifying false statements from among true statements about pictures featuring daily life in Japan.

雨なら どうしよう?
Making weekend plans, listening to a weather forecast and deciding which is the best plan. ✪

Asking visiting Japanese exchange students to write diary entries, reading, then writing a brief response and reading aloud in class.

Watching a video of a Japanese TV weather forecast and discussing the gist/details.

せかいの 天気よほう
Listening to a world weather report and completing the details on a chart. ❑

せんしゅうの できごと
Listening to accounts of the previous week's highlights and writing a summary with a partner. ✪

Activity-type 4
Giving information

Group diary
Adding a sentence to a class diary in which each learner makes a comment about the day.

What's on this week
Writing a 'Forthcoming Events' column, e.g. featuring parties, concerts, weekend activities.

Giving brief spoken accounts of the day's events and experiences to peers.

Giving a brief impromptu spoken account of the events of the weekend.

Aesthetic

Activity-type 5
Making a personal response

Reading an outline of an event and writing the ending.

Writing an account of a 'special day', e.g. based around an interesting stimulus picture.

Activity-type 6
Personal expression

Writing a daily journal, e.g. recording events, feelings, thoughts, people.

Selecting an event in the future and writing about the day as if it has happened.

Module checklist

Key functions and notions	Suggested language exponents

Asking and giving information about:
- daily life

毎日何時に（ね）ますか。
たいてい（十時はん）に（ね）ます。

（けさ）何時に（おき）ましたか。
（七時）に（おき）ました。

- daily events

（けさ）、何をしましたか。
（7時）に（おき）て、（シャワーをあび）ました。それから...

- daily requests

学校の（あとで）（ミルクをかっ）てください。

- completion of an action

もう（れんしゅう）は（おわり）ましたか。
いいえ、まだです。
まだ（おわっ）ていません。

もう、（しゅくだいをし）ましたか。
はい、もうしました。
いいえ、まだ（し）ていません。

- the weather
  - now

今日の（お）天気はどうですか。
とてもいい（お）天気です。
今日はほんとうに（あつい）です。
きおんは（20）どです。

  - from a weather forecast

（7）時の天気よほうです。
かくちの天気です。

（あした）の（お）天気はどうでしょうか。
（はれ）時々（くもり）でしょう。
（はれ）のち（くもり）でしょう。

  - as it has become or may become

（ごご）から（あたたかく）なります。
（もう）（あつい）です。
だんだん（あつく）なるでしょう。

Interacting on the telephone

（メリーさん）はいますか。
はい、おまちください。
いますよ。
いま、いません。

じゃ、またあとでかけます。

Seeking, giving and denying permission

（金曜日）に（メリーさんのパーティーに行っ）ても
いいですか。
（うん）、いいです。
（行っ）てもいいです。
いいえ、だめです。
（行っ）てはいけません。

Describing a sequence of events

まず、....。そして....。それから....。さいごに....。

24 hours 二十四時間

Suggested kanji for recognition

時々、雨、天気、毎日、今、今日

Around the school
学校あんない

Stage 2　Module 3

Module objectives

Learners should be able to:

- listen to a variety of spoken texts for specific information about school life, e.g. instructions, subjects, events, travel;
- engage in and sustain a short conversation about school life and school events, e.g. school rules, sport and recreation, comparisons;
- give a short talk about school life, e.g. routines, favourite subjects and reasons, friends;
- read letters and simple brochures about school for specific information, e.g. subjects, activities, facilities;
- write about school life in a letter to a prospective exchange student, e.g. about study, topics of interest, school life;
- write a short personal school journal;
- write information about school life which could be included in a school information brochure, e.g. calendars, maps, posters, menus.

Other learning experiences
(may be conducted in English)

- Organising a 日本語会 (Japanese Club) at the school. Meetings could be held around themes, e.g. music, food, magazines.
- Presenting a display on school life in Japan, e.g. in the school library or entrance foyer.
- Discussing school life in Japan, e.g. にゅうがくしけん and school duties, with an exchange student or Japanese visitor.

Suggested units of work

- My school day
- A school in Japan
- School information brochure

Suggested activities

Interpersonal

Activity-type 1
Interacting and discussing

Writing a letter to a pen friend or sister school describing school life, e.g. location of school, subjects, rules, events, feelings about school.

Interviewing other learners about typical school routines, e.g. travel, time taken, homework, extra-curricular activities.

ユニフォーム
Drawing and labelling a school uniform for a Japanese pen friend or describing a photo of self in a school uniform. ✪

Role-play
Interviewing the school principal, canteen operator, teachers or parents about school life.

Discussing the pros and cons of wearing a school uniform.

Identifying teachers from spoken descriptions, e.g. この先生はせがたかくて たいていジーンズをはい ています。だれでしょう？

アンケート！
Surveying class members on favourite pop groups, canteen or snack food, lunchtime or after school activity, etc. to include in a brochure for a sister school. ❑

Activity-type 2
Interacting to get things done

としょかんはどこ？
Pair work: Incomplete Maps: Asking questions to complete both maps of a school, e.g. 受付（うけつ け）のとなりに 何があり ますか。❑

Making decisions with a partner to complete an ideal school timetable.

Pairwork
Asking questions to complete gaps in a school timetable, e.g. a modified Japanese school timetable.

Informational		Aesthetic	

Activity-type 3
Getting information and using it

Activity-type 4
Giving information

Activity-type 5
Making a personal response

Activity-type 6
Personal expression

さぶろうくんの学校
Looking at a modified Japanese school brochure for specific information, e.g. times, timetable, clubs. ✪

Listening to exchange students making simple speeches about school life, school friends, and asking questions or discussing in English.

「オアシス」 'Oasis'
Reading the items in a modified school paper for gist and specific details. ✪

学校のしせつ
Listening to descriptions of school facilities and matching to pictures. ❑

クラブかつどう
Listening to short descriptions of school club activities and guessing to which club the speakers belong. ✪

わたしの学校で
Listening to accounts of daily school life and completing a chart. ❑

Creating a list of reasons to explain lateness, homework not done, etc., and placing in the class.

School rules
Making a list of school rules, e.g. for visitors' information. ❑

Writing and presenting a speech about school, e.g. for delivery in Japan.

Making a calendar of school events, e.g. to send to a sister school.

Producing a labelled map of the school, e.g. for visitors' information (bilingual or Japanese).

Listing teacher's instructions in Japanese.

Making an ideal menu for the school canteen.

Writing a report on a school event.

Writing a homework journal, e.g. days, subjects, times, feelings.

Using pictures of Japanese schools, listing similarities and differences.

Writing short impromptu accounts of the day's experiences at school.

Using pictures of Japanese schools, writing a comparative account of similarities and differences for inclusion in the school magazine.

Writing an account of the first day at high school (or primary school), e.g. what learners did, what it was like.

Creating a class book with pictures, photos with humorous captions and articles, e.g. to send to a sister school.

Writing a poem or cartoon about a school identity.

Designing a poster to advertise or promote a school event.

Module checklist

Key functions and notions	**Suggested language exponents**

Asking and giving information about:
● daily travel

（家）から（学校）までどうやって（来）ますか。
（たいてい）（バス）で（来）ます。
でも、時々あるいて（来）ます。

（学校）までどのぐらいかかりますか。
（20分ぐらい）かかります。

いくらぐらいかかりますか。
（一ドル）ぐらいかかります。

● when things happen

（学校）は何時から何時までですか。
（八時はん）から（三時はん）までです。

● subjects and activities

どんな（かもく）を（勉強し）ていますか。
（英語や日本語やしゃかいかやびじゅつなどを
勉強し）ています。

どの（クラブ）に入っていますか。
（テニスクラブ）に入っています。
クラブに入っていません。

● school population

（生と）が（何人）ぐらいいますか。
（七百人）ぐらいいます。

● events

（りくじょうきょうぎたいかい）はいつですか。
（ぶんかさい）は何月何日ですか。
（十月二十日）です。
（十月二十日）にあります。

Asking about and identifying

この／その／あの（たてもの）は何ですか。
（図書館）です。

（クラブ）の名前は何と言いますか。
（　　）と言います。

Asking for and stating preference

どんな（かもく）が一ばん（好き）ですか。
一ばん（おもしろい）（かもく）は何ですか。
（びじゅつ）です。

Asking for and giving reasons (for a preference)

なぜ（好き）ですか。
（しゅくだい）が（おおい）からです。
（先生）が（おもしろ）くないからです。
（先生）が（しんせつ）だからです。
（先生）が（しんせつ）じゃないからです。

Describing what is not allowed

（図書館）の中では（たべ）てはいけません。
（ちょうれい）の時は（はなし）てはいけません。

Around the school　学校あんない

Key functions and notions	Suggested language exponents

Suggested kanji for recognition

図書館、中、勉強、来る、分、言う、英

Money
もらったお金で

Stage 2　Module 4

Module objectives

Learners should be able to:

- listen to a variety of spoken texts for specific information about money, e.g. shopping, part-time jobs, saving;
- engage in and sustain a short conversation about money, e.g. how it is spent, part-time jobs;
- give a short spoken presentation about money and spending, e.g. preferences, pocket money, part-time jobs;
- develop and present a short role-play featuring a money matter, e.g. requesting a loan from a parent;
- read magazines, advertising brochures and signs to extract gist and specific details, e.g. about goods, prices, what is being promoted;
- write a series of connected sentences to promote something, e.g. a product, a shop, a part-time job.

Other learning experiences

(may be conducted in English)

- Finding out about the そろばん, e.g. what it looks like, how and when it is used.
- Researching お年玉（おとしだま）、おせいぼ and おちゅうげん, when these are given and why.
- Discussing exchange rates and their impact on travellers to and from Japan.
- Discussing which companies use Japanese images and Japanese 'culture' to promote the sale of their goods in Australia and which Japanese influences are being used.

Suggested units of work

- Part-time jobs
- Clothing and fashion
- Shopping in Japan

Suggested activities

Interpersonal

Activity-type 1
Interacting and discussing

Game
Playing 'I went shopping and I bought...' using classifiers, e.g. 1st learner: えんぴつを三本買いました。2nd learner: えんぴつを三本とねこを一ぴき買いました。

アンケート：アルバイト
Surveying other learners about part-time jobs, e.g. type of work, how often and how much is earned. Results are tabulated and displayed. ❑

Guessing the job
Asking and answering questions about a mystery part-time job (questions can only be answered with yes or no).

Conducting a survey
Finding the most popular make and colour of car, clothing shop, dream holiday destination, etc.

24人に聞きました：アルバイト
Discussing information presented in a survey about part-time jobs, hours worked and payment received. ✪

Group discussion: Deciding what to be, given a list of jobs and conditions, e.g. salaries, holidays, travel opportunities.

Activity-type 2
Interacting to get things done

Role-play
Taking roles, e.g. customer, sales staff, parent, child, and purchasing various goods such as clothing, books, magazines, groceries or electrical goods.

Role-play
Given a choice of restaurants, movies or other entertainment alternatives, deciding where to go, what to do and what to buy, within a budget.

Role-play
Asking and answering questions at the information counter, e.g. where and on what floor an item is located, where toilets can be found, when shop closes.

おねがいします....
Role-play: Convincing a parent that you need money for... ✪

Imagining you and a friend have won an amount of money and talking with a partner about how it will be spent.

Informational		Aesthetic	

Activity-type 3
Getting information and using it

Reading Japanese magazines and grouping items by categories, e.g. goods only available in Japan, goods similarly priced in Australia, goods which are cheaper/more expensive than in Australia.

買ったもの
Listening to shop conversations and finding out what was bought, the quantity purchased, and the cost. ❏

「本日休業」
Identifying simple notices often found in Japanese shops, e.g. 本日休業 (ほんじつきゅうぎょう) 'Closed Today'. ✪

どのアルバイトがいい？
Listening to people talk about their interests and matching each to a suitable part-time job. ✪

こうこく
Reading advertising material and extracting details, e.g. about price, shop, colour. ✪

Activity-type 4
Giving information

Giving a short talk about a part-time job, e.g. when and where someone works, saving goals, weekly purchases and preferred shops.

Writing a brochure promoting local shops, providing information for Japanese visitors, e.g. a map, commentary of a walk around a group of shops, suggestions of places not to miss, times.

Looking at Japanese fashion magazines or local versions, choosing a complete outfit and describing it.

Writing brief accounts of things learners want to save for and using pictures to illustrate.

Keeping a record of how money is spent, e.g. the total amount spent by each class member, per week, on junk food.

おかいけいひょう
Designing and using a sales docket for taking orders during role-plays. ❏

Activity-type 5
Making a personal response

買ってほしい！
Writing a response to an advertisement, e.g. from a local newspaper or magazine. ✪

Activity-type 6
Personal expression

Creating a piece of advertising material, e.g. a store catalogue, showing pictures of products, prices and brief descriptions.

Designing a poster to promote a new range of products, e.g. at the school canteen.

ちゅうい！
Writing a warning about an inferior or harmful product.

Role-play
A memorable experience in a shop.

Module checklist

Key functions and notions

Asking for and giving information about:
- money and pocket money

- part-time jobs

- reasons for doing something

- price

- purchases

- location (of a shop)

- availability

Suggested language exponents

おこづかいをもらいますか。
ええ、もらいます。
いいえ、もらいません。

だれにもらいますか。
（りょうしん）にもらいます。

いつもらいますか。
（毎週金曜日）にもらいます。

月に何かいもらいますか。
（３）かいぐらいもらいます。

おこづかい／アルバイトのお金で何をしますか。
（ふく）や（カセット）などを買います。
ちょきんします。

アルバイトをしていますか。
はい、しています。
いいえ、していません。

どこでアルバイトをしていますか。
（　　）の（大きいスーパー）でしていますか。

週に何かいアルバイトをしていますか。
週によってちがいます。
ふつう、（２）かいします。

週に何時間アルバイトをしていますか。
（８）時間ぐらいしています。

いつアルバイトをしていますか。
（学校のあとで）（４時）から（９時）までします。

ぜんぶでいくらですか。

どんな物を買いたいですか。
何を買いたいですか。
（ジーンズ）を買いたいです。どこがいいですか。
（あのみせ）がいいですよ。

（ゆうびんきょく）はどこですか。
（えき）はどこにありますか。
（まっすぐ行って、つぎのかどを右にまがって、左）
がわです。
（２かいのエレベーターのとなり）です。
（２かいのエレベーターのとなり）にあります。

このへんに（きっさてん）がありますか。
ありますよ。

Money もらったお金で

Key functions and notions

Suggested language exponents

Interacting in a shop

いらっしゃいませ。
かしこまりました。
しょうしょうおまちください。

Requesting quantities of things

（えはがき）を（一まい）ください。
（200円のきってを２まいと160円のきってを５まい）
ください。

Suggested kanji for recognition

買う、買い物、週、お金、右、左

Holidays
休暇（きゅうか）

Stage 2   Module 5

Module objectives

Learners should be able to:

- listen to a variety of spoken texts for information about holidays, e.g. activities, arrangements, impressions;
- engage in and sustain a short conversation about holidays, e.g. plans, alternatives, weather, impressions;
- give a short spoken presentation about a holiday, e.g. a day-by-day itinerary;
- read holiday itineraries and journals to extract gist and specific details, e.g. about places, events, impressions, comparisons;
- write a short illustrated journal about a holiday, including factual information and personal impressions;
- write a response to a holiday picture or photo, e.g. what is good and bad about the place featured, memories, activities.

Other learning experiences
(may be conducted in English)

- Discussing the similarities and differences between holidays in Japan and Australia, e.g. school holidays, amount of holidays taken, employee holidays.
- Discussing the extent of Japanese tourism in the state and/or local area, e.g. collecting and discussing brochures, newspapers and maps produced for Japanese tourists in Australia.

Suggested units of work

- Planning a holiday
- Holiday journal
- A holiday in Japan

Suggested activities

Interpersonal

Activity-type 1
Interacting and discussing

インタビュー：休み
Interviewing other learners to find out about a holiday, e.g. where they went, impressions, etc. ❏

日本での休み
Discussing Japanese festivals and cultural events and matching descriptions to pictures. ✪

Asking learners about favourite holidays and ranking the 'Top 10'.

Writing a postcard to a friend, describing a holiday.

Role-play
Telephoning from a holiday destination and chatting, e.g. about the weather, events, impressions.

Referring to a holiday photo album, answering a partner's or teacher's questions, e.g. ここはどこですか。この人はだれですか。ここで何をしましたか。

Activity-type 2
Interacting to get things done

Given a list of possible items to take on various holidays, deciding on the most important, e.g. for a hiking weekend.

Role-play
Telephoning a friend to arrange a holiday, e.g. where to go, what to take, what the weather might be like.

どのへんですか
Role-play: Using a map, asking the way to a particular destination while on holiday in Japan. ✪

Given a spending budget, looking at a list of weekend or holiday activities and deciding with a partner what to do.

休みのスケジュール
Completing a travel schedule from several incomplete ones. ❏

Informational		Aesthetic	
Activity-type 3 Getting information and using it	**Activity-type 4** Giving information	**Activity-type 5** Making a personal response	**Activity-type 6** Personal expression

<table>
<tr>
<td>

とうきょうについて
Listening to a conversation about attractions in Tokyo and summarising the main details. ✪

Reading simplified holiday brochures for specific information, e.g. price of accommodation, cost of meals, distance to nearest public transport, local attractions.

しんじられない
Reading holiday postcards, drawing pictures to suit the given information and writing a reply. ❑

よみましょう
Reading magazine articles and making a list of familiar words and expressions. ✪

</td>
<td>

Writing and illustrating a 'Holidays in Australia/ Japan' wall chart, e.g. giving the names, dates and popular activities related to holidays such as クリスマスデー、おぼん、母の日.

Presenting an illustrated talk about a holiday, e.g. using a holiday photo album.

Designing and writing a brochure featuring a particular holiday attraction or destination.

Writing a few sentences, e.g. about Christmas Day, ゴールデンウィーク、お正月, to include in the school newsletter or information bulletin.

Writing a journal of a holiday, e.g. an illustrated 夏休みのにっき.

Giving a short talk about a holiday in Japan, e.g. using *Japan Foundation Slide Bank*: 12か月シリーズ.

Presenting short spoken accounts of things to do in the local area during holidays.

Presenting short reports on cheap and enjoyable weekend (or holiday) activities.

</td>
<td>

Bringing a magazine picture of a holiday destination and writing the advertisement to accompany the picture.

Reading extracts from simplified stories, e.g. 「たなばたさま」、「びんぼうがみとふくのかみ」and discussing the gist in English.

Using a picture of a Japanese holiday scene or attraction, writing an account of how a character spent a holiday there.

</td>
<td>

Writing a paragraph entitled 'My Ideal Holiday'.

Writing advertising jingles for a holiday destination, event or attraction.

</td>
</tr>
</table>

Module checklist

Key functions and notions	Suggested language exponents
Asking and giving information about activities, e.g. during holidays	（休み）に（何をし）ましたか。 （ともだちの家）に（行っ）て、（ビデオをたくさん見）ました。 （えいがに行っ）たり、（買い物をし）たりしました。 （日本）へ行きますか、（シンガポール）へ行きますか。 （日本）へ行きます。 何もしません！ どこに／へも行きません！
Asking about and describing impressions	（たのしかった）ですか、（つまらなかった）ですか。 （キャンプ）も（パーティー）も（たのしかった）です。
Asking for and making comparisons	（何）が一ばん（たのしかった）ですか。 （りょこう）が（一ばん）（たのしかった）です。
Asking about and making arrangements	（お休み）に（何をし）ましょうか。 （まち）へ（行っ）て、（買い物をし）ましょう。 どうやって（行き）ましょうか。 （何）にのって（行き）ましょうか。 （バス）にのって行きましょう。
Asking about and describing plans	もうすぐ（夏休み）です。（何をする）つもりですか。 （りょこうする）つもりです。 何をする事にしましたか。 （日本へ行く）事にしました。
Narrating a sequence of events	一日目は...。つぎの日は...。 さいごの日は...。
Giving reasons	（日本）は（たのしかった）です。だから、また（行き）たいです。 （こわかった）です。だから、もう（のぼり）たくないです。
Expressing surprise	へええ！ すごい！ ほんとう！ しんじられない！
Hesitating	あのう... ええと...

Holidays 休暇(きゅうか)

Key functions and notions	Suggested language exponents

Suggested kanji for recognition

食べ物、飲む、お茶、お正月、海、一日目、今／先／来週

Homestay in Australia
日本からのお客様

Stage 2　Module 6

Module objectives

Learners should be able to:
- listen to a variety of spoken texts for information about the home and home life, e.g. rooms, contents, family routines, duties;
- engage in and sustain a short conversation about home and home life, e.g. home duties, directions to nearby shops;
- give a short spoken presentation about home and home life;
- read a variety of written passages about home and home life for specific details, e.g. things allowed at home and not allowed;
- write brief notes and messages for a homestay guest, e.g. where and how to feed a pet, how to get to a friend's house;
- write an account of a real or imagined visit of a homestay guest, e.g. their experiences, experiences of the host family.

Other learning experiences

(may be conducted in English)
- Discussing what to be aware of when staying with a family in Japan or hosting a Japanese guest, e.g. no shoes worn inside, washing dishes under hot running water, different voltages.
- Making a list of the types of souvenirs, foods, shops and attractions appreciated by Japanese visitors, and making this information available to future host families.
- Discussing a Japanese home, e.g. にわ、たたみ、ざぶとん、こたつ、げんかん.

Suggested units of work

- Before the homestay guest arrives
- In and around my house
- My homestay guest

Suggested activities

Interpersonal

Activity-type 1
Interacting and discussing

Writing and inviting a Japanese student to stay in Australia, including an introduction of self and family.

Discussing topics of mutual interest with a visitor from Japan, e.g. sports, after-school activities, home life.

日本からのおでんわ
Role-play: Talking on the phone with a friend from Japan about the friend's forthcoming visit to Australia, e.g. arrival date, likely weather, what to bring. ✪

Using a floor plan of own home, explaining the layout to a visitor, e.g. ここはわたしのへやです。となりに...

Introducing a homestay guest to friends at school.

Role-play
Explaining to a guest, e.g. what the family typically eats, where they eat, when they have a barbecue, how often they eat in front of TV.

Writing a 'Welcome' or 'Farewell' card for a guest.

Role-play
Introducing a guest to the host's family and asking questions about the guest's own home life.

Activity-type 2
Interacting to get things done

Writing and inviting an exchange student, e.g. to a barbecue, go shopping, and suggesting what to wear, what to take, travel arrangements, etc.

Role-play
Taking a guest to the school shop or canteen and helping them, e.g. to buy lunch, buy school books.

Planning an outing with a homestay guest and arranging transport, times, what to wear, etc.

Deciding what ingredients to buy for Japanese cooking and where to buy them.

ぜひもってかえってね！
From pictures of items a homestay guest wants to take back to Japan, completing a chart showing cost, where to buy, which to post, etc. ❑

Informational		Aesthetic	
Activity-type 3 Getting information and using it	**Activity-type 4** Giving information	**Activity-type 5** Making a personal response	**Activity-type 6** Personal expression

Informational

Activity-type 3
Getting information and using it

Listening to a visitor's 「じこしょうかい」 then asking questions, e.g. いつオーストラリアにつきましたか。どのぐらいいますか。オーストラリアはどうですか。どんなりょうりが好きですか.

たのしいけいけん
Listening to homestay guests talking about their experiences (good and bad) in Australia and making a summary. ✪

どこへ
Reading directions and finding out where a homestay guest has gone. ✪

Activity-type 4
Giving information

Writing a weekly roster of family duties, e.g. for display in the kitchen.

かぞくのマナー
Writing a list of things people are expected to do and not do in the house, such as when the TV, video, stereo, telephone can be used. ❏

わすれないで！
Writing short messages for a homestay guest, e.g. where and how to feed a pet, where to meet a friend and what to take, what to take on an excursion. ✪

Writing and presenting a speech welcoming a Japanese visitor.

Writing an account of a homestay guest's experience in Australia, e.g. a journal of their visit.

Writing a brief itinerary for an outing with a homestay guest, e.g. places to visit, times, transport, meals, things to do.

Aesthetic

Activity-type 5
Making a personal response

Writing a story based on the photos learners have taken during the visit of an exchange student or Japanese group.

Activity-type 6
Personal expression

Imagining being a visitor from Japan and writing a letter to a friend in Japan about a stay in Australia, e.g. after going to first barbecue, during the last week before returning to Japan.

Module checklist

Key functions and notions	Suggested language exponents

Welcoming and farewelling someone

こんにちは。（　）さんですね。
ああっ！　いらっしゃい！
げんきでね。
また、ぜひ来てください。

Asking for and giving information about:
- areas of the house

ここは（だれのへや）ですか。
（　）さんのです。
ここは（あね）の（しんしつ）で、ここは（おふろば）です。

- areas and their functions

（ここ）で（ともだちとあそび）ます。

- home contents

これは（だんろ）で、これは（まき）です。

- the location of items

すみません、（おふろば）はどこですか／にありますか。
（げんかん）の（そば）です／にあります。

- meal times and other routines

（あさごはん）はたいてい（何時）に（食べ）ますか。
（学校がある日）は（7時）ごろ食べます。

- directions

（ここ）から（ゆうびんきょく）はどうやって行きますか。
まっすぐ行って、つぎのかどを（左）にまがって、
（右）がわです。
（右）にあります。
まっすぐ行って、すぐ（左）がわです。

- distance

（ここ）から（町）まで、どのぐらいかかりますか。
（バス）で（20分）ぐらいかかります。

Seeking, giving and denying permission

（せんたくもの）はじぶんで（あらっ）てもいいですか。
ええ、いいですよ。
ええ、（ここ）で（あらっ）てください。

（10時）まで（でんわをつかっ）てもいいですか。
こまりますよ。（9時）まではいいです。

（ここ）で（食べ）てもいいですか。
（ここ）で（食べ）ないでください。

Arranging things to take

（ピクニック）に（何）をもって行きましょうか。
（ソーセージ）と（パン）をもって行きましょう。
（セーター）を（もって行っ）たほうがいいです。

Reminding someone

（でんしゃのお金）をわすれないで！
（住所）をわすれないでください。

Key functions and notions	Suggested language exponents

Suggested kanji for recognition

客、道、町、住所

Variety show
バラエティー
ショー

Stage 2   Module 7

Module objectives

Learners should be able to:

- listen to short spoken texts for a variety of information, e.g. about people, interests, events;
- ask and answer simple quiz questions, e.g about attractions in Japan, Australian and Japanese lifestyles;
- give a short spoken presentation as part of a variety show, e.g. a sports report, a new foods report, a humorous weather forecast;
- write a short script for an item in a variety show, e.g. a fashion report, a local area report;
- watch a spoken presentation and make several sentences in response, e.g. what the presentation was like, what the presenter was like, reasons (simple) for comments.

Other learning experiences
(may be conducted in English)

- Listening to contemporary Japanese songs, or other music of interest to learners and discussing in English.
- Watching a Japanese game show or variety show and discussing in English.
- Listening to simple talks from people who have seen recent Japanese variety shows or other shows of interest to learners, and discussing in English.

Suggested units of work

- Developing the variety show
- Putting on the show

Suggested activities

Interpersonal

Activity-type 1
Interacting and discussing

インタビュー：今日のお客様
Role-play: Interviewing a 'personality', e.g. with questions about Australia or Japan, their 'personal' life. ❑

Role-play
Movie review: interviewing 'studio guests' about current movies, e.g. what the movies are like, what they are about, what 'rating' they should receive.

学校チャレンジ
- In teams, answering questions and, if correct, making a selection on the まるとばつ (noughts and crosses) board.
- はい、いいえ！
  Asking questions, e.g. おとこの人ですか。おんなの人ですか。せが高いですか。毎日テレビで見る事ができますか, answering with はい or いいえ and trying to guess the identity of the mystery person. ✪

せかいのりょこう
Answering questions about world geography in order to move around on a world map. ❑

Activity-type 2
Interacting to get things done

Role-play
Telephoning a contest winner, e.g. asking about their personal background, how they will use the prize, how they feel.

Role-play
Candid camera: Using the dress-up box and props, interviewing people on the street about an amusing topic or theme question such as さしみを食べるのが好きで すか。こんばん、デートをしましょうか.

Listening to reviews of the week's 'Top 10' rental videos and deciding which ones to see.

しょうたいしましょう
Writing and reading and deciding which people might be suitable to participate, e.g. in a TV chat show, talent show or quiz show. ✪

Informational

Activity-type 3
Getting information and using it

ニュースの
おもなこうもく
Listening to short news headlines and drawing pictures to suit the information. ✪

In pairs or small groups, matching descriptions of personalities to pictures.

Watching an episode from a sub-titled Japanese TV drama, identifying familiar language and discussing other language that learners were able to identify, e.g. by guessing, remembering.

Listening to the answers people give to quiz questions about Australia and Japan and selecting the correct alternative.

Activity-type 4
Giving information

Developing and presenting segments of a variety show, e.g.

- Show Host: Introducing the segments and the performers, then responding on behalf of an audience, e.g. つぎは「にんきコーナー」です。はい、～さん、おねがいします。…みなさん、はくしゅをおねがいします。
- ニュースコーナー
  Presenting an item of 'news', e.g. an event or place, who was there, who did what, comments people expressed.
- りょうりコーナー
  Presenting a talk on a favourite dish, e.g. what it's called, made from, where they eat, how often, why they like it.
- スポーツコーナー
  Presenting a report on a local or school sporting event, e.g. best players, venue, weather, player comments.
- チャンピオンコーナー： Giving a profile of a 'champion' personality, e.g. background, achievements, qualities, interests.
- 天気よほう： Presenting a humorous weather forecast.
- 'Hot Seat'
  Selecting a topic at random and talking for one minute.

Aesthetic

Activity-type 5
Making a personal response

Fill in the story
Listening to the beginning of a story or incident and completing the missing details, e.g. わたしはのどがかわきました。 だから...

Singing Japanese songs or doing a Japanese dance, e.g. ぼんおどり.

Giving short spoken responses to the items presented in the variety show, e.g. what the segment was like, simple reasons for the comments made.

Activity-type 6
Personal expression

Using the dress-up box and a range of props, presenting the segments of the variety show (see Activity-type 4).

Viewers' Faxes
Using a theme, designing a single page for a Viewers' Fax Contest, with the class selecting one according to criteria, e.g. most humorous, most unbelievable.

Writing or talking about what learners expect to be doing when they are, e.g. 18 years old, 35 years old, 60 years old.

Module checklist

Key functions and notions	Suggested language exponents

Asking and giving information about:
- Australian and Japanese lifestyle

（日本人）は（おふろの中でせっけんをつかい）ますか。
いいえ、（つかい）ません

- distance, travel time

（オーストラリア）から（東京）まで、（ひこうき）で（どの）
ぐらいかかりますか。
（10時間）ぐらいかかります。

- time and actions

（　）さんはいつ（オーストラリアにつき）ましたか。
（12日のあさ、8時につき）ました。

- leisure and entertainment activities

（ひまな時）、（何をする）事が好きですか。
（ひまな時）、（何をする）のが好きですか。
（スポーツをし）たり、（おんがくを聞い）たり
する（事／の）が好きです。

Asking about and quoting direct speech

（　）さんは何と言いましたか。
「　　　」と言いました。

Enquiring about and expressing likes and dislikes

（ケーキ）は（何が）好きですか／きらいですか。
（エクレア）が一番好きです／きらいです。
（お茶）は好きですか、きらいですか。
まあまあです。

Enquiring about and giving reasons

なぜ（好き）ですか。
どうして（好き）ですか。
（チョコレートがだい好きだ）からです。
（　）さんが（おもしろい）から（好き）です。

Enquiring about and giving impressions

（レストラン）はどうでしたか。
（おいし）くて、（たのしかった）です。
（レストランはきれい）で、（りょうりはおいしかった）
です。

（これ）をどう思いますか。
（高い）と思います。
ちょっと（へん）だと思います。

どうでしたか。
（上手）に（うたい）ました。
（おもしろ）く（話し）ました。
（あまり上手）に（でき）ませんでした。

Introducing a speaker or performer

はじめのかたは（　）さんです。
（スピーチ）です。だいは「　　」です。
（　）さん、よろしくおねがいします。

Responding to a talk or performance

（　）さん、たいへん（おもしろかった）です。
みなさん、はくしゅをおねがいします。

Variety show バラエティーショー

Key functions and notions	Suggested language exponents

Suggested kanji for recognition

東京、山、富士山、京都、話す、思う

What happened this year?
今年のでき事

Stage 2　Module 8

Module objectives

Learners should be able to:

- listen to short spoken texts and make a simple written summary, e.g. of the main details, the gist of the story, the person's main concerns or feelings;
- engage in and sustain a short conversation about the year's events, e.g. experiences, future and holiday plans;
- give a short spoken presentation about an event during the year, e.g. a school trip, a visit to a restaurant;
- read journals and reports of the year's events and summarise the main details, e.g. people involved, highlights, reasons for the writer's opinions;
- write an article for a school magazine featuring the year's activities, e.g. people, events, personal achievements, future intentions;
- write a short poem about one of the year's events.

Other learning experiences
(may be conducted in English)

- Writing articles about visiting Japanese students, e.g. exchange students, study tour groups, sporting groups, and including these in the school magazine (in English).
- Looking at Japanese magazines, discussing them and noting ideas for learners' own magazine.

Suggested units of work

- This year at school
- Our magazine
- The best thing for me this year was . . .

Suggested activities

Interpersonal

Activity-type 1
Interacting and discussing

In groups, discussing and making notes summarising the year's activities and highlights, then writing up and presenting to the class, e.g. 1 月に . . . そして、2 月に . . . etc.

Exchanging accounts of the year's events (e.g. from group activity above) with a sister school and publishing the results in a magazine.

'The class of . . .'
Placing photos of the class or year's events on a sheet and writing comments, e.g. about the people featured, events, experiences, impressions, messages.

てがみ
Reading letters in Japanese magazines and writing replies. ✪

Writing a class letter to a sister school in Japan (or Australia) and publishing the letter and the reply in a magazine.

インタビュー：
今年のでき事
Interviewing each other, a visitor or school personality about one of the year's events and featuring the interviews in a magazine. ❏

Activity-type 2
Interacting to get things done

Interviewing class members about their personal highlights of the year, e.g. holidays, social events, a personal achievement.

Discussing and making a list of the 'Top 7' events of the year.

In small groups, preparing a simple report of major events during the year which have caught people's attention, e.g. a major world conflict, a school issue or event.

日本のりょうり
Deciding which Japanese dishes to prepare (e.g. for a class party) and who will provide the necessary ingredients. ✪

Informational		Aesthetic	

Activity-type 3
Getting information and using it

今年のゲスト
Reading interviews with 'famous' personalities, summarising the main points and using the information to write a magazine article. ✪

だれが言っている
でしょう？
Putting learners' names in a hat, selecting one and writing a 'quote' that the selected learner often makes. Reading one at a time, learners try to guess identities. The quotes could be retained and featured in a class magazine.

Listening to class members giving accounts of the year's events and experiences and summarising their main points.

Welcome Station
Reading letters of introduction from people wanting homestays in Japan and summarising the information provided. ✪

「ライブ＆パーティー」
Reading an advertisement for a party and finding the details. ✪

Activity-type 4
Giving information

Creating puzzles for inclusion in the school magazine, e.g. 'The odd one out', crosswords, 'Who am I?'.

Writing accounts of things which have been 'in fashion' and 'out of fashion' during the year, e.g. including reasons.

Making a written summary of the year's best and worst events or experiences.

Making a list of personal resolutions for next year, including reasons (simple).

Writing a 'Teacher Feature', including topics such as likes, dislikes, personal details and favourite sayings, etc.

Writing and presenting a short spoken summary of the year's memorable events.

Writing and recording accounts of the year's events on audio tape and keeping for classes in future years.

Activity-type 5
Making a personal response

Looking at a photo or picture of an interesting school event for 2 minutes then writing as much about the picture as possible, from memory.

Story building.
Given a list of words or points related to an interesting school incident or event, expanding on the words to write a short paragraph.

Writing entries for a caption competition.

Writing a short poem in response to a picture or photo of one of the year's events.

Activity-type 6
Personal expression

Writing *cinquain* poems
In groups or as a class, creating simple poems within a framework:
Line 1: Stating the subject in a single word, often a noun, e.g. ふゆ.
Line 2: Describing the subject in two words, usually an adjective and a noun, e.g. つめたいかぜ.
Line 3: Describing an action about the subject in three words, e.g. いきています、ふいています、とんでいます.
Line 4: Expressing an emotion about the subject in four words, e.g. あし、ゆび、みみがいたい！
Line 5: Restating what has already been said using another single word, e.g. さむい！

Using a range of greeting cards (including Japanese cards, if available), designing and producing Christmas and New Year cards in Japanese.

Writing a short poem based on one of the year's events or experiences.

Module checklist

Key functions and notions

Suggested language exponents

Asking for and giving information about:
* proficiency and achievements

今年どんな事がありましたか。
（日本語）が（上手）になりました。

（漢字）はどうですか。（上手）になりましたか。
ええ、（上手）になりました。
いいえ、まだ上手じゃないです。

* events and activities

（どの休み）が一番（よかった）ですか。
そうですね。
（秋休み）が一番（楽しかった）です。

（春休み）に（何をし）ましたか。
（日本に行っ）て、（富士山を見）たり、
（おすしを食べ）たりしました。
（あそん）だり、（りょこうし）たりして、（楽しかった）
です。

（１月）に学校がはじまりました。
（そして）、（２月）はすごくあつかったです。

* future intentions

また、（日本に行き）たいですか。
ええ、また（行く）つもりです。
いいえ、もう（行き）たくないです。

* simple explanations

（はこね）は（何）で（有名）ですか。
（みずうみ）で（有名）です。

（しんじゅ）で（有名）ですか。
いいえ、（おんせん）で有名です。

Explaining an inevitable outcome

（病気）で（りょこうに行き）ませんでした。
（病気）で（行く）事ができませんでした。

Asking for and giving simple reasons

なぜ（日本に行き）たいですか。
（富士山にのぼり）たいから（行きたい）です。

なぜ（日本に行き）たくないですか。
（じしん）が（おおい）から（行きたくない）です。

What happened this year　今年のでき事

Key functions and notions	Suggested language exponents

Suggested kanji for recognition

有名、漢字、楽しい、病気

Appendices

Appendix 1
Related Resources

The resources given below may be of assistance to teachers implementing Stage 1 and Stage 2.

Course books

Alfonso, A., *Alfonso Japanese Book 1*, Curriculum Development Centre (CDC), Canberra, 1976.

Alfonso, A., Gotoo, S. & Hoaas, S., *Alfonso Japanese Book 2*, CDC, Canberra, 1978.

Bunka Institute of Language, *Bunka Shokyuu Nihongo (1)*, Tokyo, 1989.

Burnham, S. & Saegusa, Y., *Kimono Nihongo Level 1 Workbook*, CIS Educational, Melbourne, 1990.

Burnham, S. et al, *Kimono Nihongo Level 2*, CIS Educational, Melbourne, 1991.

Burnham, S. & Saegusa, Y., *Kimono Nihongo Level 2 Workbook*, CIS Educational, Melbourne, 1991.

Jet Program, *Japanese Language Text: Beginning Level Book One*, Conference of Local Authorities for International Relations (CLAIR).

Lee, M., *Isshoni*, Moreton Bay Publishing, Brisbane, 1989.

Lee, M., *Isshoni Book 2*, Moreton Bay Publishing, Brisbane, 1991.

McBride, H., *Kimono Nihongo Level 1*, CIS Educational, Melbourne, 1990.

Nozomi, T., *NHK Nihongo Kooza: Japanese Elementary Course 1st Step*, Japan Broadcasting Company, Tokyo, 1989.

Pegasus Language Services, *Basic Functional Japanese*, The Japan Times, Tokyo, 1987.

Rowell, A. & Hall, L., *Konnichi Wa*, Jacaranda, Brisbane, 1989.

Saka, K. & Yoshiki, H., *Nihongo Kantan, Speak Japanese: A Textbook for Young Students*, Kenkyusha, Tokyo, 1988.

Tasmanian Education Department, *Alfonso Japanese: Supplementary Materials, Book 1*, CDC, Canberra, 1989.

Williams, L., *Active Japanese 1*, Longman Paul, New Zealand, 1990.

Williams, L., *Active Japanese 2*, Longman Paul, New Zealand, 1990.

Williams, L., *Active Japanese 3*, Longman Paul, New Zealand, 1991.

Yoshida, I., *Japanese for Beginners*, Gakken, Tokyo, 1976.

Supplementary materials

Colombia, *Kodomo No Uta*, (songs), Tokyo, (CBY-756, 757, 758 — 3 audio tapes).

Education Department of South Australia, *Alice in Japan*, Educational Production Services, Adelaide, 1983.

Evans, M., *Activity Based Learning*, Association of Independent Schools, Brisbane, 1990.

Evrat-Jones, A., *Dekiru Kana: An Activity Book for Students of Japanese*, PCS Publications, Toowoomba, 1990.

Evrat-Jones, A., *Dekiru Kana: Teacher Guide*, PCS Publications, Toowoomba, 1990.

Galet, D., *Even Monkeys Fall From Trees and other Japanese Proverbs*, Tuttle, Rutland, Vermont, 1987.

Hajimete No Kotoba Bideo, Kodansha, Tokyo, 1985.

Hinder, P., *Let's Eat Out*, The Japan Times, Tokyo, 1988.

Hyoojun Romaji Kai, *All-Romanized English–Japanese Dictionary*, Tuttle, Tokyo, 1973.

Isogai, M., *Joyful Tokyo*, Nichido Kikaku Company, Tokyo, 1985.

Japan As It Is, Gakken, Tokyo, 1985.

Japan Graphic Incorporated, *Japan Pictorial*, Tokyo.

Japanese Language Year 7 Resource Kit, Curriculum Support Branch, New South Wales Department of Education, 1990.

JNTO, *Make Friends For Japan*, Nissei International Publishing, Tokyo, 1988.

Kaneyoshi, N., *Pictorial Encyclopaedia of Japanese Culture: The Soul and Heritage of Japan*, Gakken, Tokyo, 1987.

KEK Kokusai Kooryuukai, *Experiencing Japanese Culture — An Activities Based Approach*.

Kimono Nihongo Level 1 Cassettes, CIS Educational, Melbourne, 1990.

Kimono Nihongo Level 1 Teacher's Manual, CIS Educational, Melbourne, 1990.

King Record Co., NHK, *Minna No Uta*, (songs) Tokyo, (K10H-4449, 4450 — 2 audio tapes).

Konna Toki Nihongo De (video), Nihon Terebi, Bunka Jigyoodan, Tokyo, 1988.

Machida, T. & Taguchi, M., *Japanese for Children*, Melbourne, 1980.

Makino, S. & Tsutsui, M., *A Dictionary of Basic Japanese Grammar*, The Japan Times, Tokyo, 1986.

Martin, S., *Basic Japanese Conversation Dictionary*, Tuttle, Tokyo, 1982.

Mitamura, Y., *Let's Learn Hiragana: First Book of Basic Japanese Writing*, Kodansha, Tokyo, 1985.

Mitamura, Y., *Let's Learn Katakana: Second Book of Basic Japanese Writing*, Kodansha, Tokyo, 1985.

Mizutani, N., *Nihongo Karuta: A game for students of Japanese*, Bonjinsha, Tokyo, 1988.

Mizutani, O. & Mizutani, N., *Nihongo Notes (1 to 8)*, The Japan Times, Tokyo, 1987.

Mizutani, O., *How to be Polite in Japan*, The Japan Times, Tokyo, 1987.

Motohashi, F. & Hayashi, S., Tsuda Center for Japanese Language Teaching, *24 Tasks for Basic Modern Japanese Volume 1*, The Japan Times, Tokyo, 1989.

Motohashi, F. & Hayashi, S., Tsuda Center for Japanese Language Teaching, *24 Tasks for Basic Modern Japanese Volume 1 Cassette Tape*, The Japan Times, Tokyo, 1989.

Murray, D. & Wong, T., *Noodle Words*, Tuttle, Tokyo, 1977.

Nemoto, M. & Yashiro, E., *Hirokosan no Tanoshii Nihongo*, Bonjinsha, Tokyo, 1986.

Popham, P., *Insiders' Guide to Japan*, CFW Publications, Hong Kong, 1987.

Quackenbush, H. & Ikeda, S., *Katakana in 48 Minutes*, CDC, Canberra, 1989.

Quackenbush, H. & Ohso, M., *Hiragana in 48 Minutes*, CDC, Canberra, 1983.

Sakade, F., *A Guide to Reading and Writing Japanese*, Tuttle, Tokyo, 1976.

Sakata, Y., Sakuma, K. & Althaus, M., *Let's Learn Japanese: A Television Course, Basic I*, Kenkyusha, Tokyo, 1986.

Scarino, A., et al *Australian Language Levels (ALL) Guidelines Books 1, 2, 3 and 4*, CDC, Canberra, 1988.

Takahashi, H., *Takahashi's Pocket Romanized Japanese-English Dictionary*, Taiseido, Tokyo, 1984.

Tasmanian Education Department, *Asia Wise*, Hobart.

The Japan Foundation Slide Bank: Seikatsu Series.

The Japan Foundation Basic Japanese-English Dictionary, Bonjinsha, Tokyo, 1986.

Vale, D., Scarino, A. & McKay, P., *Pocket ALL: A Users' Guide to the Teaching of Languages and ESL*, Curriculum Corporation, Melbourne, 1991.

Yamaguchi, M. & Kojima, S., *A Cultural Dictionary of Japan*, The Japan Times, Kenkyusha, Tokyo, 1979.

Yamashita, H., *Irasuto Katto*, Seibundoo Shinkoosha, Tokyo, 1986.

Yokoyama, N., *Yokoyamasan No Nihongo*, Nihongo Kyooiku Sentaa, Tokyo, 1989.

The place of games

Games can provide meaningful and quite intense language practice. Games can also encourage learners to sustain interest in their study of Japanese as well as provide meaningful contexts for using Japanese.

An increasing volume of material on language games is being written and it is recommended that teachers refer to this when considering and selecting games.

Factors to consider:

- Is the game for drilling, language practice or language use?
- Is it a listening, speaking, reading or writing game?
- Does the emphasis in the game serve the intended purpose?
- What level of teacher control is required?
- What are the rules and instructions?
- What is the level of error correction and competition?

The games below are suitable for Stage 1 and Stage 2 learners.

Dictionary games

Learners use a dictionary with entries in hiragana to:

- find the page(s) where particular words are located;
- find the first page where words beginning with a particular hiragana appear;
- find the word listed before or after a given word.

Happy families

Learners form groups of four. For each group of players, two sets of 16 pictures are needed. A player shuffles and deals out the cards, placing them face down. Players sort their cards into families. If they have a complete family they place it face down in front of them. The first player asks another for a card he/she needs to make up a family. If the player who is asked has the card in question it is handed over and the player has another turn. If they do not have the card the process is reversed. The first player to complete one (or an agreed number of) family/families is the winner.

Concentration

Collected pictures (e.g. foods, drinks, sports) are pasted on to cards. The equivalent Japanese words are written on other cards. Learners turn over cards to find matching pairs.

Bingo

Cards containing 9 (or 16) items in squares are distributed to the class. As an item is called (by the teacher or a member of the class), participants who have the item on their card mark it (or cover it with a counter, etc.). Once a participant completes a row (in any direction) or an entire card, he or she calls 'Bingo!' and wins the game.

Bingo can also be played using a variety of numerals and classifiers (e.g. times, quantities, dates) as well as categories of vocabulary (e.g. foods, drinks, subjects, sports).

Shopping bag

Select a category of goods and divide learners into three groups, e.g. 'apples', 'grapes' and 'pears'. Learners sit on chairs in a circle and a caller standing in the middle calls one of the items (in which case all in that group must stand and swap chairs). The last person standing becomes the new caller.

Guessing the word

Paste magazine cut-outs or draw pictures on cards to represent words or expressions. Learners select cards and others try to guess which one by asking questions which are responded to with はい or いいえ until the card is guessed.

ほんとう／うそ！

Learners write five truths and one lie about themselves (e.g. length of time studying particular subjects, birth sign, zodiac, personality and capabilities). Other learners ask questions to find out the lie.

だれでしょう？

A caller tries to guess the identity of a mystery person in the class or group (known to the rest of the class) by asking a question, e.g. If this person was a food, what food would they be?

Other learners suggest answers within the given category until the caller can guess the learner's identity. The caller can select a further category by asking another question, e.g. のみもの だったら、何ですか。どうぶつだったら、何ですか.

Guessing who

Learners write three things about themselves, the teacher reads one out and other learners guess who it is.

Appendix 3
Songs

The place of songs

Songs are an important language resource and provide many opportunities for learner and teacher interaction. Listening to or singing songs frequently involves repetition of highly rhythmical phrases, and catchy and memorable words which can do much to facilitate language acquisition.

Songs can also act as a stimulus for role-plays and other forms of personal expression such as poetry (reading and writing) and creative writings. Learners may also enjoy writing Japanese words to well-known English songs.

The following songs may enhance learners' enjoyment of their language learning as well as reinforce language activities in the various modules.

Stage 1

Module 1   How do you do?
よろしく
グッドバイ (Goodbye)
あ、い、う、え、お (Vowel song)
もしもし (Telephone song)
しあわせならてをたたこう (If you're happy)

Module 2   Family and friends
かぞくととともだち
はやおきどけい (Family song)
なかよしこみち (Good friend)
こんにちはあかちゃん (Hello baby)

Module 3   Things about me
じぶんのこと
きらきらぼし (Twinkle, twinkle, little star)
やまのおんがくか (I am a musician)

Module 4   Free time
フリータイム
たこたこあがれ (Song of kites)
おもちゃのチャチャチャ (Cha Cha Cha toys)
こいのぼり (Boys' Day song)
ひなまつり (Girls' Day song)
もういくつねると (New Year song)

Module 5   Neighbourhoods
きんじょ
あかあおきいろ (Traffic lights)
しずかなこはん (Quiet lakeside)

Module 6   The four seasons
四季（しき）
はるがきた (Spring has come)
ゆうひ (Sunset)
うみ (Sea)
はるのおがわ (Spring stream)
あめふり (Rain)
さくら (Cherry blossoms)
はるよこい (Spring, come!)
てるてるぼうず (Rain, rain, go away)
まつぼっくり (Pine cone)

Module 7   Welcome
いらっしゃいませ
おはよう (Good morning)

Stage 2

Module 1   People
人々
しろいブランコ (White swing)
わかものたち (Youngsters)

Module 2   24 Hours
二十四時間
しきのうた (Song of the four seasons)

Module 3   Around the school
学校あんない
がくせいじだい (School days)

Module 5   Holidays
休暇（きゅうか）
スキー (Skiing)

Module 6   Homestay in Australia
日本からのお客様
ふるさと (Home town)

Module 8   What happened this year
今年のでき事
ほたるのひかり (Auld lang syne)

Appendix 4
Programming support materials

Sample units of work

Each module contains a number of suggested units of work (titles). A unit of work is envisaged as a short-term 'unit' within the module, covering a number of lessons or weeks.

Units of work have been selected from each of Stage 1 and Stage 2 and exemplified here for teacher reference:

- Stage 1, Module 1: All about us and First steps with Japanese script;
- Stage 2, Module 1: That's the story of my life.

The samples use the layout of the pro forma (provided on pages 132/133) which may be of assistance to teachers when developing units of work.

Please note: The samples do not show complete programs. They have been provided to indicate how teachers might approach their programming, and how the pro forma might be used.

Unit of work

Stage _____1_____ Module _____1_____

Unit of work title _All about us and First steps_

with Japanese script

Duration _3–4 lessons_

Class _8A_

Module objectives

Learners should be able to:
- follow short, very explicit spoken instructions requiring short verbal or physical responses;
- greet people at school using high frequency learned patterns and responses;
- introduce themselves and others (name only);
- read familiar words in hiragana.

Other learning experiences

(may be conducted in English)
- Discussing the three Japanese writing systems
- Discussing how English words have been 'borrowed' in Japanese
- Discussing how language is dynamic, e.g. how slang expressions come in and out of fashion in both Australia and Japan

Assessment activities

- Role-playing A introducing B to C
- Creating a design or page border using Japanese characters
- みなさん, きいてください
  Listening to classroom commands and matching to pictures

Activities and exercises

Having learners copy out own name in katakana and recognise it from teacher flashcards. Learners to make own name cards, these are randomly distributed and learners circulate around class identifying their own card and greeting the holder.

Introducing hiragana for はい、こんにちは、さようなら.

Learners responding to taking of class roll with はい and greeting and farewelling others around them.

Doing listening comprehension activity しゅっせきです.

Showing how to ask someone's name and giving own.

Playing a memory game with each new participant greeting and naming all previously introduced learners.

Extending introductions and drilling in pairs.

Introducing hiragana for おはよう、せんせい、みなさん、めいし、わたし、おなまえ.

Introducing further greetings, apologies and introduction of others.

Having learners participate in role-plays of A introducing B to C.

Functions, notions, language exponents (grammar)	Other (resources, sociocultural items)
Greeting others, leave taking: こんにちは。〜です。 〜さん、さようなら。 みなさん、こんにちは／おはようございます。 せんせい、こんにちは／おはようございます。 Responding to class roll call: しゅっせきをとりましょう。(recog. only) 〜さん！ はい。 〜さんはけっせきです。(recog. only)	S-cult: • writing systems • politeness, e.g. さん • how English names have been 'Japanised' (e.g. トム、バネサー) and how English sounds are changed to their most approximate equivalent Res: • flashcards of learner's names • practice name sheets • hiragana/katakana charts for learners • *Hiragana in 48 Minutes* • hiragana and katakana charts for wall H/work: Learners cut out jumbled hiragana words for はい、こんにちは、さようなら、and glue to sheet in correct order.
Asking for and giving information about name: おなまえはなんですか。 わたし／ぼくは〜です。 〜さん、こんにちは／おはようございます。 Introducing self: はじめまして。わたしは〜です。わたしのめいしです。どうぞよろしく。 Greeting others, apologising: こんばんは／おやすみなさい。 おそくなってすみません／すみません。 おげんきですか。 はい、げんきです。 Introducing self and others: 1 （３）さん、こちらは（２）さんです。 2 はじめまして。わたしは（２）です。わたしのめいしです。どうぞよろしく。 3 こちらこそ、どうぞよろしく。	S-cult: Politeness, e.g. おなまえ. S-cult: • めいし — use and design, • bowing: male and female methods, when used as greeting, apologising, in shops, etc. Some people even bow when talking on the telephone! The importance of the degree of the bow and the length of time taken. Res: • めいし worksheet • real めいし • *Hiragana in 48 Minutes* • flashcards of greetings H/work: Learners take a familiar dialogue (e.g. *Kimono* cartoon story), highlight familiar words and count up the number of times each word appears.

Unit of work

Stage ___2___   Module ___1___

Unit of work title That's the story of my life

Duration 6–8 lessons

Class 9D

Module objectives

Learners should be able to:
- listen to a piece of descriptive information about someone and summarise what is heard;
- engage in and sustain a short conversation about people;
- write a personal profile.

Other learning experiences

(may be conducted in English)
- Discussing the personalities and lifestyles of characters in the video series 「ヤンさんと日本の人々」 and noting any stereotypical characters which emerge
- As above for other videos available
- Discussing the characters which learners remember from Japanese movies they have seen (some of the discussion may take place in Japanese)

Assessment activities

- Role-play: Using the 'dress-up box', meeting someone at a party and comparing likes, dislikes and interests.
- Blind date application form: Filling in an application form including name, age, birth place, birth date, どし, likes, interests, hobbies, capabilites, future career and nationality, to appear on the TV show (to be held in class in several weeks).
- School reporter: Listening to じこしょうかい and writing short summary sentences for the school magazine.
- Role-play: Interviewing a new student about their personal background, interests and capabilities, and suggesting a school club for them to join.
- Writing a personal history of self (or other person of interest). May be presented to class or video recorded.

Activities and exercises

Introducing personal interests:
～さんはどんな事が好き
ですか。 and ～さんは
どんな食べ物／スポーツ／
かもくが好きですか。

Learners asking five friends questions and recording their responses.

Introducing and revising vocabulary for hobbies.

Surveying class to determine most popular hobbies/interests.

Drilling vocabulary for capabilities, eg.
できます and level of skill, e.g. じょうず、へた.

Introducing (or revising) adverbs, e.g.
すこし、よく、とても、あまり、
ぜんぜん、ほんとうに.

Learners receive a chart, interview a partner, record responses and write out information in full sentences.

	すこし	よく	あまり	ぜんぜん	etc.
テニス					
すいえい					
ギター					

Giving learners a set of likes, dislikes and capabilities and finding a 'perfect match'.
or
Giving learners a set of likes, dislikes and capabilites and having them seek a job from another who has a list of job requirements.

Functions, notions, language exponents (grammar)	Other (resources, socio-cultural items)
Asking for and giving information about personal interests: 〜さんはどんな事が好きですか。 〜事が好きです。(Introduce a limited number of items *as vocabulary*, e.g. テレビを見る事、えいがに行く事、かいものをする事.) Note: 本をよむ事＝どくしょ、てがみをかく事＝ぶんつう. Revision: どんな〜がすきですか。(たべもの、スポーツ、のみもの、かもく) 〜が好きです。 Responding: わたしも〜が好きです。 ああ、そうですか。 わたしは〜が好きじゃないです。 Asking for and giving information about hobbies/personal interests: しゅみは何ですか。 〜です。 あなた／〜さんは？ わたしのしゅみは〜です。 (エアロービックス、コンピューター、じょうば、etc.)	S-cult: Japanese students participate in school club activities (often every day until late), many then go to じゅく (cram school). Students may have traditional hobbies and interests, e.g. けんどう、おちゃ、しょどう, or more 'western' interests, e.g. tennis, brass band, photography. Res: flashcards for activities, foods, interests, etc. Res: flashcards for hobbies H/Work: Revise likes/dislikes and hobbies vocab. for test.
Asking for and giving information about capabilities: 〜ができますか。 はい、〜ができます。 いいえ、〜ができません。 (スキー、すいじょうスキー、テニス、からて、etc.) Asking for and giving information about degree: 〜がよくできますか。 はい、よくできます。 いいえ、すこしできます。 いいえ、あまり／ぜんぜんできません。	Res: chart Res: Information gap sheet for each student giving likes, hobbies, interests and capabilities *or* job requirements (in terms of the above).

Unit of work

Stage _____ Module _____

Unit of work title _____

_____

Duration _____

Class _____

Module objectives

Learners should be able to:

Other learning experiences

(may be conducted in English)

Assessment activities

Activities and exercises

Functions, notions, language exponents (grammar)	Other (resources, sociocultural items)

Appendix 5
Assessment support materials

The following blackline masters are provided to support assessment. They may be photocopied or adapted as required. Samples of their use can be found in the chapter on assessment.

- General objectives checklist
- Learning skills checklist
- Self-assessment form
- Progress card
- How well am I doing?
- Listening and speaking
- Reading and writing

General objectives checklist

Name _____ Class _____ Date _____

I can/_____ can: seldom   always

-   ⊢—⊥—⊥—⊥—⊣

- ⊢—⊥—⊥—⊥—⊣

- ⊢—⊥—⊥—⊥—⊣

- ⊢—⊥—⊥—⊥—⊣

- ⊢—⊥—⊥—⊥—⊣

- ⊢—⊥—⊥—⊥—⊣

- ⊢—⊥—⊥—⊥—⊣

- ⊢—⊥—⊥—⊥—⊣

- ⊢—⊥—⊥—⊥—⊣

- ⊢—⊥—⊥—⊥—⊣

- ⊢—⊥—⊥—⊥—⊣

Learning skills checklist

Name _____ Class _____ Date _____

I can/_____ can: seldom   always

- ●   └──┴──┴──┴──┘

- ●   └──┴──┴──┴──┘

- ●   └──┴──┴──┴──┘

- ●   └──┴──┴──┴──┘

- ●   └──┴──┴──┴──┘

- ●   └──┴──┴──┴──┘

- ●   └──┴──┴──┴──┘

- ●   └──┴──┴──┴──┘

- ●   └──┴──┴──┴──┘

- ●   └──┴──┴──┴──┘

- ●   └──┴──┴──┴──┘

Self-assessment form

Name _____ Class _____ Date _____

Activity:

What I have achieved:

Difficulties I encountered:

Strategies for improvement:

Progress card

Name _____   Class _____

	Checked by me	Checked by a partner	Checked by my teacher
	Date		

I can/_____ can:

-
-
-
-
-

How well am I doing?

Name _____ Class _____ Date _____

Working by yourself or with a partner, mark with a tick the pictures which show what you can do. In your notebook, write down some strategies you could use to improve your performance.

Listening and speaking

Name _____ Class _____ Date _____

Activity

	もっと がんばりましょう	たいへん よくできました

Receptive (listening)

☐ level of support required to understand, e.g. prompting, repetition

☐ degree to which learner understood important details of what was said

☐ degree to which learner understood the gist of what was said

☐ degree to which learner coped with unpredictability, e.g. change in topic, unfamiliar words

Productive (speaking)

☐ accuracy of what was said, e.g. grammar, vocabulary

☐ intelligibility of pronunciation

☐ socio-cultural appropriateness of what was said

☐ range and variety of language used

☐ degree to which learner attempted to go beyond their very familiar language range

☐ degree to which learner used strategies to sustain communication

☐ degree to which learner's speech 'flowed', e.g. within sentences, between sentences

☐

☐

☐

☐

Reading and writing

Name _____ Class _____ Date _____

Activity

	もっと がんばりましょう			たいへん よくできました

Receptive (reading)

☐ level of support required to understand the
written information

☐ degree to which learner understood important
details of what was written

☐ degree to which learner understood the gist of
what was written

☐ degree to which learner coped with unpredictable
or unfamiliar written words

Productive (writing)

☐ accuracy of what was written, e.g. grammar,
vocabulary

☐ socio-cultural appropriateness of what was written

☐ range and variety of language and script used

☐ degree to which learner attempted to go beyond
their very familiar language range

☐ degree to which learner's writing 'flowed', e.g.
within sentences, between sentences

☐

☐

☐

☐

☐

☐

Glossary of terms

Activities-based syllabus   A syllabus in which the activity is seen as the central unit of teaching and learning, and the activity-type as the central organising unit for syllabus design.

Activity   An activity involves purposeful and active use of language where learners are required to call upon their language resources to meet the needs of a given communicative situation.

Activity-type(s)   The ALL Project's six activity-types represent broad categorisations of activities, and hence broad categories of language use. Activities are categorised into activity-types according to the communication goals that they realise. The six activity-types cover the range of language use which should be promoted in the language classroom.

Assessment   The practices and procedures for monitoring and measuring learners' performance in relation to the goals and objectives of the course.

Background-speaker   A learner who has a home background in the target language.

Communication strategies   Strategies which are used to organise and maintain communication. Communication strategies may be receptive and/or productive.

Communicative data   The range of information in the target language which is used as a basis for classroom activities.

Criterion-referenced assessment   The practice of measuring a learner's performance against specified criteria. The aim of criterion-referenced assessment is to ascertain whether learners are able to carry out specific tasks. This form of assessment can be compared with norm-referenced assessment where a learner's performance is measured against the performance of another learner or group of learners whose scores are given as the norm.

Dimensions of language use   Activities are grouped in broad dimensions of language use. It is proposed that three basic dimensions of language use are relevant to the majority of school language learners: an interpersonal dimension, an informational dimension and an aesthetic dimension.

Exercise   An exercise focuses on one or more elements of the communication process in order to promote learning of the items of language, knowledge, skills and strategies needed in communication activities. Exercises can be shaping exercises or focusing exercises. *Shaping exercises* are exercises which develop and structure language within an extended piece of discourse (e.g. cloze exercises, substitution tables, matching exercises, dictation, etc.). *Focusing exercises* are exercises which focus on

elements of the communication process (forms, skills and strategies).

Exponents   The language items (vocabulary, structures) needed to realise functions, e.g. the function 'asking for directions' might entail the following exponents: 'bank', 'harbour', 'museum', 'can you tell me where X is, please?', 'where is X?'

Function   The purpose for which an utterance or unit of language is used. A function is often described as a category of behaviour, e.g. requesting, apologising, getting things done, making arrangements, expressing abuse, etc.

Genre   A particular class of speech events. Examples of genres are: prayers, sermons, conversations, songs, speeches, poems, letters and novels. They each have particular and distinctive characteristics.

Goals   The five broad categories of language learning goals which reflect the objective needs of school language learners who pursue their language learning through the ALL Framework of Stages. The five broad categories are communication goals, socio-cultural goals, learning-how-to-learn goals, language and cultural awareness goals, and general knowledge goals.

Learning-how-to-learn skills   Skills which enable learners to take responsibility for their own learning, and to learn how to learn. Learning-how-to-learn skills include specific listening, speaking, reading and writing skills.

Modes of language use   A term used to refer to individual macroskills (listening, speaking, reading and writing) or combinations of macroskills (conversation, correspondence) used to carry out a particular activity.

Notions   Meanings and concepts that learners need in order to communicate, e.g. duration, time, space, etc.

Objectives   Objectives are derived from goals. They refer to what learners are expected to be able to do at the end of a given period of instruction. Objectives may be general or specific. *General objectives* state what learners will be able to do in terms of language use for a purpose, e.g. 'Learners will be able to invite Japanese visitors to a picnic'. *Specific objectives* state what learners need to be able to do in order to achieve a general objective, e.g. 'Learners will be able to use the formal register', 'Learners will be able to ask for a reply to an invitation'.

Organisational focus   The grouping of activities for syllabus design or programming purposes, e.g. activities may be grouped under a particular theme, topic, skill, genre, literary genre, project, text, topic from another curriculum area, or a combination of these focuses.

Productive skills   Speaking and writing skills.

Program   A description of the planned learning of a class, group or individual learner over a given period of time.

Receptive skills   Listening and reading skills.

Reception   (meaning varies between States) K, P, R, Yr 1.

Skills   Refers in the main to cognitive processing skills and learning-how-to-learn skills (which include specific listening, speaking, reading and writing skills). Note: the four macroskills (listening, speaking, reading and writing) which are often given prominence in language syllabuses as the units of organisation, and combinations of them, are described in the *ALL Guidelines* as modes of language use; the unit of organisation in an ALL syllabus is the activity-type.

Socio-cultural data   Information about the social and cultural aspects of a community.

Target language   The language which is being learnt.

Unit of work   A short-term program of work; the activities in the unit of work may be integrated by an organisational focus. A long-term program is likely to be made up of a series of units of work which aim, collectively, to achieve the goals set out in the long-term program.

Based on the 'Glossary of Terms' in the *ALL Guidelines*, Book 4, pages 35–39.

Australian Language Levels (ALL) Guidelines

The development of the National Curriculum Guidelines for Japanese was fully informed by the *ALL Guidelines* and the other publications of the ALL Project. The ALL Project offers a national approach to language teaching and learning. There are fifteen books in the series.

Scarino, A., Vale, D., McKay, P., Clark, J. *ALL Guidelines Book 1 Language Learning in Australia*; *ALL Guidelines Book 2 Syllabus Development and Programming*; *ALL Guidelines Book 3 Method, Resources, and Assessment*; *ALL Guidelines Book 4 Evaluation, Curriculum Renewal, and Teacher Development*, Curriculum Development Centre, Canberra, 1988 (available through Curriculum Corporation, Melbourne).

The *ALL Guidelines* present a coherent model for the design of school-based language curriculum. They draw extensively on the latest research and developments in the teaching and learning of languages.

McKay, P., Scarino, A. *ALL Manual for Curriculum Developers*, Curriculum Corporation, Melbourne, 1991.

This book, effectively Book 5 of the *ALL Guidelines,* gives guidance for curriculum developers applying the ALL curriculum framework, and discusses the issues that have arisen from the ALL curriculum framework since the publication of the *ALL Guidelines.*

McKay, P., Scarino, A. *ESL Framework of Stages: An Approach to ESL Learning in Schools, K–12*, Curriculum Corporation, Melbourne, 1991.

A developmental, staged description of teaching objectives and activities for ESL learners K–12 based on the ALL curriculum framework. Placement procedures are included.

Scarino, A., Vale, D., McKay, P. *Developing Language Syllabuses and Programs: Stages A–C of a K–12 Series of Syllabus Exemplars — Italian*; *Stages B–D of a K–12 Series of Syllabus Exemplars — Italian*; *Stage 1 of a K–12 Series of Syllabus Exemplars — Italian*; *Stage 2 of a K–12 Series of Syllabus Exemplars — Italian*; *Stage 3 of a K–12 Series of Syllabus Exemplars — Italian*; *Stage 4 of a K–12 Series of Syllabus Exemplars — Italian*; *Stage 5 of a K–12 Series of Syllabus Exemplars — Italian*, Curriculum Corporation, Melbourne, 1991.

A set of syllabuses (seven books) following the ALL curriculum framework. Italian is used, but the syllabuses are designed as exemplars for the application, with refinement, of the ALL curriculum framework to all languages, including ESL.

Scarino, A., Vale, D., McKay, P., Wichmann, K. *ALL Inservice Facilitators' Handbook*, Curriculum Corporation, Melbourne, 1992.

An inservice manual providing guidance, references, OHTs, and handouts for a professional-development course on the *ALL Guidelines.* This publication draws on the professional-development experiences of the ALL team over five years.

Vale, D., Scarino, A., McKay, P. *Pocket ALL: A User's Guide to the Teaching of Languages and ESL*, Curriculum Corporation, Melbourne, 1991.

Pocket ALL is an overview for teachers of the key components of the *ALL Guidelines* incorporating the further thinking on the ALL curriculum framework since the publication of the *ALL Guidelines.*